OR DEATH.

OF AVENGERS.

the   *first year*

H-MEN,

NATION have landed on your

and ammunitions of all kinds,

The
YEAR OF LIBERTY
THE GREAT IRISH REBELLION OF 1798

1798

THOMAS PAKENHAM

Abridged by Toby Buchan

In memory of John Kane
buan-chara

TIMES BOOKS

RANDOM HOUSE

Contents

RIGHT: General Lazare Hoche, the 28-year-old commander-in-chief of the 15,000 French soldiers sent to liberate Ireland in December 1796.

OVERLEAF: Most of the French armada sent to Bantry Bay limped back in January 1797 to their bases in France. But one battleship, the **Droits de l'homme** *(left) with 600 troops under General Humbert, was intercepted off Brest by two British frigates,* **Amazon** *and* **Indefatigable** *(centre and right). The artist, John Luny, has caught the moment of high drama. After the ships had fought for ten hours in darkness, and the* **Droits de l'homme** *had been dismasted and lost 100 casualties, the moon broke through the clouds, revealing the dreaded Penmarck rocks and a lee shore. The* **Amazon** *was wrecked, but the crew got ashore and were taken prisoner. The* **Indefatigable** *weathered the rocks. The* **Droits de l'homme** *struck a reef and 400 men were drowned. But Humbert escaped to fight another day.*

PROLOGUE

On THE night of 16 December 1796, the last great French invasion force to set sail for the British Isles slipped past the British squadron blockading Brest. Five days later most of the fleet – 35 ships with 12,000 troops aboard – arrived unopposed at its destination: Bantry Bay in south-west Ireland. The French planned to invade Ireland, expel the British with the help of the Irish revolutionary party, and set up an independent Irish republic. It was to be the first step in the conquest of England, the English revolution, and the creation of an English republic modelled on France.

The prospects for the Irish part of this scheme could never have seemed brighter. There were a number of beaches suitable for landings. There was a light wind and little sea. There were no signs of hostile preparations on shore, nor any reason to believe that the British navy was on its way to intercept. Less than ninety miles away, the large military and naval base of Cork lay almost undefended. In a few days the whole of the south of Ireland could be theirs.

On board the 80-gun battleship, the *Indomptable*, was the Irishman whose irresistible enthusiasm had been the mainspring of the expedition. A pale, slightly built 33-year-old barrister, his name was Wolfe Tone.

The son of a Protestant coachmaker, Tone had won a scholarship to Trinity College, Dublin, and in due course had been called to the Irish Bar. In 1791, frustrated by the lack of professional and political prospects for someone without family connections, and dazzled by the ideas of the French Revolution, he had helped found a radical movement known as the 'United Irishmen'. Its aim was to throw open the Irish Parliament – at that time the preserve of a Protestant oligarchy – to all Irishmen irrespective of rank or religion. Initially, the movement's methods were to be non-violent. But soon after war broke out between Britain and France in 1793, the reformers became revolutionaries. The Irish Government, regarding the movement as seditious, drove it underground.

On their part, the United Irishmen recognized that they would achieve nothing without French assistance, and that France would not intervene for anything less than a complete revolution in Ireland.

Expelled to America for his political activities in 1795, Tone was asked by the United Irish organization to go to France to collaborate with the French army of liberation. He did, and succeeded brilliantly. Somehow, he had persuaded the new rulers of France – the Directory – to embark on the scheme. General Lazare Hoche, the most experienced of all French generals at that time, not excepting Bonaparte, had been appointed Commander-in-Chief.

In Bantry Bay on 21 December 1796, only one thing marred the prospects of success. As the fleet had dodged the British naval blockade off Brest, the frigate carrying Hoche had become separated from the main force, and it was agreed to delay the landing until he had caught up.

But now the extravagant good fortune that had brought them so close to triumph suddenly deserted them. For five weeks, the wind hung in the east, frustrating the British blockade, then spiriting the invasion fleet to Ireland. For one day – the 21st – the wind was light and the sea calm. In Hoche's absence, no landing was made. On the 22nd the wind inexorably freshened and in the squalls of rain and snow more than half the fleet parted company with the flagship. On the 24th, the easterly gale became a storm. Still Tone and the French staff officers with him clung to the precarious hope of a landing. The storm continued. One by one, the fourteen remaining ships cut their cables and turned for France. On the night of the 27th the storm became a hurricane.

When it blew itself out, the *Indomptable*, already damaged by a huge sea, found herself alone. As Tone put it, England had not had such an escape since the Armada.

Above: Theobald Wolfe Tone, the 33-year-old United Irish leader who persuaded the French to try to liberate Ireland.

CONS

PART ONE

Britain and Europe, January 1798 and before

*B*Y THE beginning of 1798 the King's First Minister, William Pitt, knew that the war with Revolutionary France had brought Britain to the verge of bankruptcy. And still the cost mounted: not least for the defence of Britain and Ireland against French invasion.

Ireland remained the weakest link in that defence, as the providential escape from the Bantry Bay expedition had shown. Now there were reports of dangerous unrest there. And on one score the crisis was real enough. The country was even closer to bankruptcy than Britain.

Though not insensitive to the dangers, Pitt largely left the running of Ireland to the Home Secretary, the Duke of Portland, leader of the Whig wing of the Coalition Government.

The previous year had been disastrous. Austria, Russia and Prussia had made peace with France, leaving Britain virtually without allies. At home there had been riots, mutinies, and an incipient revolutionary movement. And always at their backs was the problem of Ireland.

In 1782, weakened and humiliated by the loss of the American colonies, Britain had agreed to a new deal for Ireland. She had had no choice. An 'Irish Volunteer army' had been formed by Ireland's ruling class to protect the country against the French. Encouraged by the Americans' success, they then demanded a measure of self-government under threat of an Irish War of Independence. Thus by the new deal of 1782 the

William Pitt, Britain's war-weary Prime Minister. Ireland, he knew, was the weakest link in Britain's line of defence against France.

PIRACY

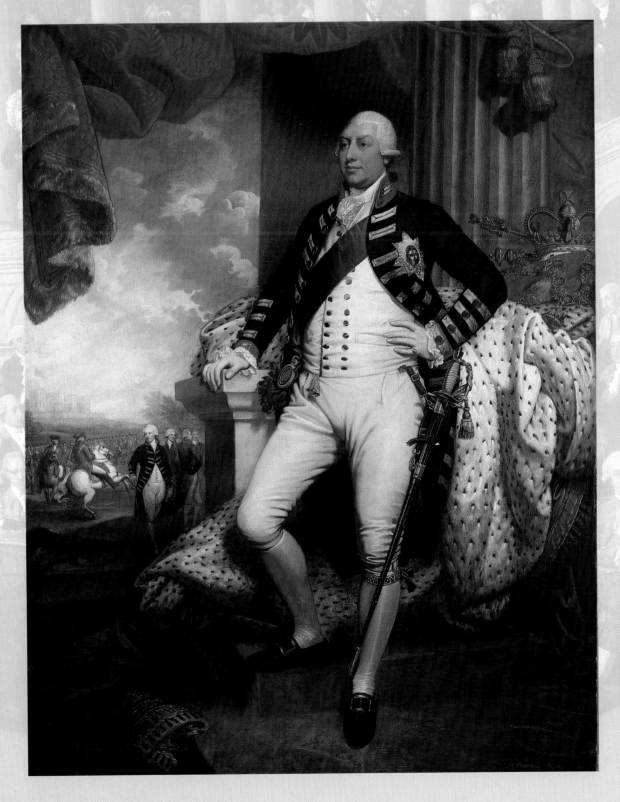

George III, King of Britain and Ireland since 1760. Humiliated by the loss of the American colonies, he had reluctantly agreed to Pitt's concessions to Irish Catholics. But he drew the line at full Catholic emancipation.

Irish Parliament was made – theoretically – equal with Westminster. At a price, an American-style revolution had been avoided.

Yet it soon became clear that the Irish problem was not resolved. The Irish Volunteer army were of the Garrison, the 'Protestant nation' of settler stock. Their national aims had nothing whatever to do with the aims of the mass of the Irish people. And Britain's concessions to this small, selfish and corrupt oligarchy had only exacerbated the grievances of the rest.

The survivors of the Catholic upper class wanted equality with their Protestant neighbours and, above all, political power, since Parliament was closed to Catholics. The emergent Catholic middle class also wanted political rights, as well as equal rights in the professions (the law was also closed to them). By giving greater power to the Irish Parliament, Britain had only increased the frustrations of those excluded from it. Still more explosive were the grievances of the peasantry, whose lives were made miserable by high taxes and an impossibly harsh land system, exacerbated by – mainly – religious differences.

Such was the ominous situation when, in 1789, France exploded into revolution. Might not the oppressed people of Ireland be the next to seek a democratic revolution?

Pitt and his Government attempted to redress the worst Irish grievances. A reluctant Irish Parliament agreed to relax most of the penal laws – but refused to grant complete emancipation by allowing Catholics the right to sit in Parliament. Nothing was done about the land system, which pinched hardest on the mass of the people. The war with France caused a slump that crippled the Irish economy. The French revolutionary cause became still more attractive.

FACING: Lord Camden, the Irish Viceroy, high-minded and humane, but utterly demoralized by trying to govern Ireland.

LEFT: Edward Cooke, under-secretary at Dublin castle. More robust than Camden, he tended to side with Camden's anti-Catholic advisers.

LEFT: Lord Castlereagh,
Pitt's 28-year-old protégé
and acting chief secretary.
Inexperienced as he was,
he had to manage the wild
Irish gentry who controlled
the Dublin Parliament.

them, everything now depended on Bonaparte.

Late in 1797, Tone and Edward Lewins, the unofficial ambassador for the Irish revolutionary movement, were granted an interview with the great man in Paris. Though this was something of an anti-climax, they returned, in January 1798, bringing a sheaf of documents detailing Ireland's condition and their plans for a revolution to establish an independent Irish republic.

Bonaparte was not encouraging. If Ireland was to be invaded as a prelude to the conquest of England, then everything – including the organizing of the underground army to rise at the right time and place – must be ready in a matter of weeks. Otherwise he would pursue his ambitions elsewhere.

The Irish exiles had no grounds for complaint in the following weeks. On 8 February Bonaparte made a rapid tour of the Channel ports, ordering transports to be prepared, and men, horses, ordnance and supplies to be embarked – all to be ready in three weeks.

A few days later these preparations were reported by a spy to London, and thence to Dublin Castle. No one could now doubt that Bonaparte was in earnest – whichever country was to be invaded.

Then, in 1797, Pitt learned of the secret Jacobin-style army in Ireland, the United Irishmen.

In France, meanwhile, a vast new invasion force was assembling at the Channel ports, its commander to be the man who had smashed the Triple Alliance and humbled the Pope – General Bonaparte, whose overriding object had become the defeat of Britain. His 50,000 veterans of the Italian campaign were now released for service elsewhere. Where better to send them, Wolfe Tone pointed out to the Directory, than to invade the weakest part of the British Isles, Ireland?

Tone and the other Irish revolutionaries in France had suffered nothing but disappointments since the Bantry Bay fiasco, including the abandoning of two other invasion attempts. For

Dublin and the South, 22 January–12 March 1798

The Viceroy of Ireland, Lord Camden, was high-minded and humane, but three years of trying to govern with a cabinet and Parliament drawn from the corrupt and selfish Irish Protestant oligarchy had utterly demoralized him.

In theory, executive power rested with the Viceroy, responsible to Pitt and the King. But the

LEFT: Lord Clare, the formidable Lord Chancellor, and one of the leaders of the informal cabinet (the 'junto') who terrorized the viceroy.

PRECEDING PAGES: The Irish Volunteers, painted here by Francis Wheatley, challenging the British Government in Dublin in 1779: 'Free trade or revolution!' By 1798 the movement had been suppressed. Some radical Volunteers, like Napper Tandy (under red flag on the left) had become United Irish leaders. But many joined the government's militia or yeomanry, like Lord Mountjoy (on white horse), who died leading his regiment in 1798.

RIGHT: *The Irish House of Commons addressed by Henry Grattan (right, standing) in 1780 during the campaign to force Britain to give Ireland free trade and legislative independence. Grattan, and many of the MPs, are wearing Volunteer uniform to show they mean business.*

RIGHT: *Charles James Fox (left), with the British radical Horne Tooke (right), caricatured in 1798 as the creatures of French democracy.*

BELOW: *Charles James Fox, leader of the Whig Opposition and Gratttan's most important ally in London. But both men had now decided that it was a waste of breath to speak in their respective Parliaments.*

ABOVE: *Henry Grattan, once the darling of the Irish Parliament but now denounced as a covert United Irishman.*

Irish cabinet, nominally only the Government's advisers, were fast becoming the country's real rulers. Dominating this cabinet were John Beresford, the elderly Commissioner for Revenue; John Foster, Speaker of the Irish Parliament; and the formidable old Lord Chancellor, Lord Clare. All had years of experience at managing British Viceroys. Once a Viceroy had shown real independence: Lord Fitzwilliam, Camden's predecessor, had sided with Henry Grattan's party, the Irish Foxites lobbying for Catholic emancipation, and sacked Beresford. He was recalled by Pitt.

Of Camden's personal staff at Dublin Castle, the Chief Secretary, Thomas Pelham, shared his despondency. More robust was Edward Cooke,

Under-Secretary for the Civil Department, although he tended to side with the cabinet. Finally, there was the Viceroy's nephew – and Pitt's protégé – the young and brilliant Lord Castlereagh. It was these men who were to be Camden's support in the impending crisis.

On 22 January Camden informed the British Government that gentlemen's houses in the Irish Midlands had been raided for arms, and their trees cut up for pike handles. Queen's County magistrates were about to ask the Viceroy to 'proclaim' the district, impose a curfew and call in the army.

Camden thought them more alarmed than was necessary. The regular army were at hand in the garrison towns. In their dual capacity as yeomanry

The Hopes of the Party! or the Darling Children of Democracy!

FACING: Lord Edward Fitzgerald, younger brother of the great Kildare magnate, the Duke of Leinster, and first cousin of Charles James Fox. According to one spy report, he was the leader of the violent party in the the United Irish Executive.

officers and magistrates, the gentlemen should be able to keep the country quiet without, effectively, declaring martial law. But, he added dejectedly, the cabinet would not resist these calls, and he would be forced to agree.

A fortnight after proclaiming Queen's County, Camden heard still worse news from the South. The only active magistrate in a vast tract between Cork and Tipperary had been savagely murdered. Then further assassinations of the few remaining magistrates were reported.

Camden took little comfort from the knowledge that for years back Tipperary and the South had often been rent by bitter agrarian wars between the land-hungry peasantry on the one hand, and the landlords and magistrates on the other. These had spread northwards, and developed into many distinct forms of violent strife. In Ulster there was not only a war between landlord and tenant, but also between two rival groups of tenants – Catholic, called Defenders, and Protestant. The Catholic peasantry in the Midlands then adopted the name Defenders.

Up to this time, the magistrates had dealt with such disturbances, but now the Irish gentry, inflamed by reports of murders, were crying for new measures of repression. Camden, however, still hesitated to introduce martial law.

The Castle maintained an extensive network of secret agents abroad, and of informers within the United movement. Their information, however, tended to be obscure or conflicting, particularly about the strength of the United organization.

The Government's best information came from a radical barrister and popular playwright, Leonard McNally, who, on 4 March, sent a report which made it clear that the revolutionary movement had reached a critical new phase.

The precise identity of the United Irish Executive was still a mystery, but the main troublemakers were known: the successful radical barrister, Thomas Addis Emmet; William McNevin and John Lawless, respected doctors; the leading Whig, John Chambers, an assistant to Grattan; John Sweetman, a Dublin brewer; Richard McCormick, secretary of the

Publish by J. Athin Corner of Castle Street April 26 1798

ARTHUR O'CONNOR *Esqr*

Drawn from the Life in Maidston Jail

ABOVE: Arthur O'Connor, Lord Edward's ally, who left for London – perhaps bound for France – 'much displeased' with a split in the Executive.

LEFT: John Sheares, radical barrister. With his brother Henry he supposedly joined the new Executive after the arrest of most of the United Irish leaders at Bond's house.

*PRECEDING
PAGES:
The port of Brest,
the naval base
from which the
French sent their
expeditions to
invade Ireland.*

*RIGHT: Napoleon
Bonaparte during
his victorious
campaign in Italy.
After Hoche's
sudden death in
1797, Napoleon
was to be the new
master of France.*

Catholic Committee; Arthur O'Connor friend of the English Whigs and nephew of Lord Longueville; and, by far the most influential, Lord Edward Fitzgerald. There were also two wealthy businessmen waiting in the shadows: Oliver Bond and Henry Jackson.

The dominant intellectuals were Emmet and O'Connor; neither, however, had the kind of qualities that capture the hearts of the people. But Lord Edward Fitzgerald did. An early convert to the ideas of Rousseau and Paine, he had served in the war in America. In 1793 he had resigned his seat in the Irish Parliament after an extraordinary outburst against the Government.

These United leaders were now agreed that only a complete break from England would give Ireland the economic rights, and her professional classes the political power, that justice demanded, and that this could only be achieved by revolution. But on the vital question of how to accomplish this, they were fatally divided.

An influential section of the Executive, led by O'Connor and Lord Edward, had announced that they believed the widespread United movement in the country was sufficiently well organized to rise without the French. Emmet, McCormick and McNevin violently disagreed. Emmet's line carried the day and O'Connor left for London, 'much displeased'. His faction, however, was still a force to be reckoned with.

Through their spies, the Government had watched the conspiracy grow from a perfectly legal society of reformers to a huge underground army committed to armed revolution. If the leaders chose their moment well, they had some chance of success; if the French joined them, then Ireland might be lost to the Empire.

Although the Government often considered arresting the leaders, the problem lay in convicting them, for most informers, including McNally, refused to let their evidence be used in court. Nevertheless, Camden was under strong pressure from the Irish gentry and their supporters in Parliament. The immensely powerful speaker, Foster, leader of the right wing, the *ultras* who still resisted the relaxation of the penal laws against the Catholics, vehemently put the case for arresting the known conspirators, even if they could not be brought to trial.

A few days later new information tipped the balance sharply in favour of Foster's plan, and Portland now reluctantly conceded that the conspirators could be arrested at Camden's discretion.

The intelligence had come from a new

LEFT: 'Britain's difficulty is Ireland's opportunity'. But was it France's opportunity? In January 1798, Wolfe Tone tried to convince Napoleon (An 1898 engraving).

informer, a young Catholic merchant, Thomas Reynolds, who had useful connections to both Wolfe Tone and Lord Edward. He had joined the movement more than a year before, but had not taken an active part. In December, however, Lord Edward, fearing the Government was suspicious of him, asked Reynolds to take his place as United colonel for County Kildare. Reynolds could hardly refuse, and was soon a member of the Leinster Provincial Executive.

When O'Connor's violent party challenged the moderates, Reynolds at last, so he said, saw the movement in its true colours. Accordingly, on 25 February, he confided to a friend, a merchant called Cope, that he knew 'someone' who could give the Government all the information they needed.

Without disclosing Reynolds's identity, Cope went immediately to Pelham, who authorized him to offer Reynolds virtually a blank cheque for the vital information. The latter now produced a copy of the actual minutes of that week's meeting of the Executive. It confirmed the Government's worst fears. The revolutionary army apparently outnumbered the Government forces by more than 5 to 1, totalling 279,896 armed men. It was also clear that the Executive were putting the finishing touches to their plans for the rising.

Camden and his advisers now devised a scheme which would enable them not only to seize the conspirators, but also, they hoped, to bring them to justice.

On 12 March, according to Reynolds, the delegates of the Leinster Executive were to meet in Dublin. Once again a motion for immediate rising, without the French, would be proposed; this time it would probably be carried.

Shortly after ten on the morning of the 12th, Town Major Henry Sirr, Dublin's notorious chief of police, surprised the Leinster Executive in conclave at Oliver Bond's house in Bridge Street. At one swoop he seized ten provincial delegates, two members of the Executive and their papers. Meanwhile, Sweetman, Emmet, Jackson and McNevin, among others, were taken.

Several of the country delegates, however, were late in arriving at Bond's, and so evaded arrest. But only two members of the Executive escaped. Richard McCormick, despairing of being able to restrain his violent colleagues, had gone into hiding, and soon fled abroad to safety, thus leaving Lord Edward, the leader of the violent party, as the sole survivor of the United Executive.

Dublin, 12–30 March

In order to prove in court that the arrested leaders were guilty of high treason the Castle needed the testimony of the – to them – unknown informer who had betrayed the meeting. But Reynolds, via Cope, refused point blank, and the problem was still unresolved when a fresh political crisis broke.

On 26 February the Commander-in-Chief in Ireland, General Sir Ralph Abercromby, had issued a general order which among other things accused the Irish army of atrocities. In mid March a copy of this order reached Pitt and Portland. Had Camden really authorized such 'a public and indiscriminate censure' of the whole Irish army, 'almost an invitation to a foreign enemy'?

Camden had seen the order; indeed, he had been attempting to hush it up. Circulated to all senior officers, it stated that the Irish army was 'in a state of licentiousness which must render it formidable to everyone but the enemy'. Commanding officers were therefore instructed to enforce the strictest discipline, and reminded that standing orders expressly forbade troops to act against the disaffected without being called on by the magistrates, unless themselves attacked.

A capable commander and an efficient and humane administrator, Abercromby had one clear aim – to rebuild the Irish army to meet the threat

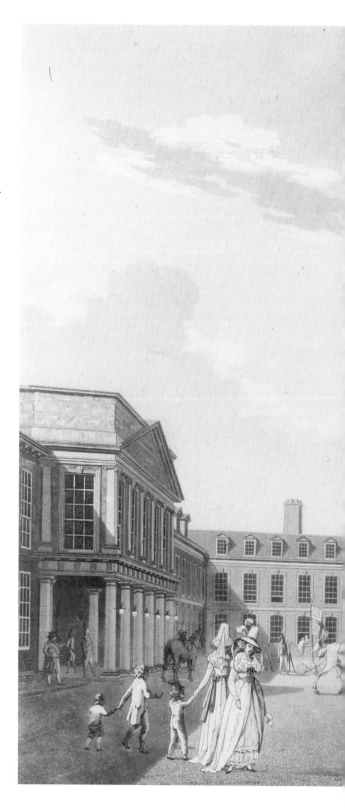

ABOVE: Dublin Castle in the 1790s, seat of the Viceroy and hub of British power. But it was a castle only in name – and quite indefensible.

OVERLEAF: Dublin harbour with the domed Custom House in the background. On the eve of the rebellion Dublin's population was estimated at 200,000, making Dublin the second city of the empire.

ABOVE: The Royal Exchange, Dublin, in the 1790s, the centre of fashionable life. Despite the threat of rebellion, the city was wide open to attack, and none of the bridges had guard-posts.

of a French invasion. The task was daunting, for it was defective in almost every military respect. Moreover, there was a 'very disgraceful frequency of courts martial', coupled with a huge number of complaints at the troops' behaviour. But the most alarming feature was the way the regular army was scattered in small detachments all over Ireland. Instead of concentrating these units in the garrison towns, from where they could be rushed to meet any attempted landing by the French, the Government had allowed over half of them to be dispersed in small parties to protect the gentry – in fact, the job of the yeomanry – in disturbed areas.

Camden had seen at once the huge damage the order could do if exploited by the Opposition in Parliament, who already contended that the army was guilty of illegal methods of repression. At a cabinet meeting, it was unanimously agreed to hush up the business.

Nothing came out until, on 14 March, Camden heard of London's alarm at the order. At a painful interview with the Viceroy next morning, Abercromby defended his actions. He had issued the order, he stated, to correct the abuses in the Irish army, and to 'stimulate the exertions of the country' – the gentry. If, however, he did not enjoy the confidence of the Irish cabinet, he would gladly resign.

Camden, who needed Abercromby, back-pedalled. But that very evening the order was leaked to the Irish papers from the London press. It was too much for the Irish army officers and the rest of the gentry. All their bitterness at what they called the Government's policy of half-measures against the conspiracy rushed to the surface.

The solidarity of the Irish cabinet was shattered. Foster formed a cabal against Abercromby, and lobbied furiously for his dismissal. London learned that both Houses of Parliament were 'in a state of smothered flame'.

Others, like Pelham, deplored this campaign, recognizing that Abercromby's remarks, however unfortunately worded, were perfectly true. But the Viceroy had at last made up his mind. He would instruct Abercromby to countermand his order; and he would lay his request to resign before the King. The political balance of power had now shifted decisively towards Foster and the party who favoured strong measures.

Meanwhile the Midlands and the South now seemed to be slipping out of Government control into the hands of the rebellious peasants. It was the same wretched story from all over Munster and nearer Dublin: attacks in broad daylight;

gentlemen robbed of their arms; more troops an absolute necessity; martial law the only solution.

The Viceroy gave in yet again. On 30 March the Privy Council declared the country to be in a state of actual 'rebellion', threatened the disaffected with the most summary measures unless they surrendered their arms, and imposed martial law over the whole kingdom.

For the time being Abercromby still commanded the army. Camden now appealed to him to go south before he gave up command and quell the outrages by disarming the disturbed districts. It was asking a great deal, yet Abercromby agreed, countermanded his own order, and left for the South.

The law was now to be put in the hands of the army, and the army in the hands of Lieutenant-General Sir Gerard Lake. And Lake believed in the reckless exercise of military power.

Dublin and the Midlands, 31 March–9 May

Two ardent young republican barristers, John and Henry Sheares, were the leading lights of the new United Executive. Hovering in the background was Samuel Neilson, imprisoned for sedition and since released on parole. But the Sheares brothers were hardly the stuff to lead a revolutionary army, and Neilson was an alcoholic. On Lord Edward were centred the hopes of the cause.

The arrests had dealt a double blow to the local branches of the movement. Not only had they lost their most active leaders, but their confidence in the Executive was shaken. Now the proclamation of martial law had dealt a crushing blow to their capability for war.

Meanwhile the Lent Assizes had started and in some places, notably Queen's County, were proving extraordinarily successful in convicting those arraigned for outrages. And, though less spectacular than those in Queen's, other assizes in the rest of the Midlands and South were satisfactory enough to the Government. Hundreds were sentenced, some to death, for their part in the disturbances.

So far so good. The leaders of the conspiracy had been arrested, the outrages punished, peace restored. It was now time to disarm the rank and file of the movement. Instead of taking individual suspects and prising from them, by any method, information about concealed weapons (as Lake had done in the North the previous year), Abercromby planned to use collective punishment. If all else failed, troops would be sent to live at 'free quarters' in the disturbed areas – with powers to requisition food, stock, fodder and so on. Punishment would

ABOVE: General Lake, the heavy-handed English general who succeeded Abercromby as Irish commander-in-chief. Lake believed in 'prompt punishment' and 'salutary shocks'.

be systematic, not indiscriminate, 'to excite terror' and so 'obtain our end speedily'. But as little actual force as possible was to be used.

Within a few days of each other the first ultimatums expired; Tipperary first, then Leinster's adjoining counties – Kildare, King's and Queen's.

In Queen's County the free quarters began on 22 April – with amazing results. Nearly all the stolen firearms were recovered, as well as hundreds of pike heads. At the end of a week good order was 'miraculously restored'. The gentry regained their confidence.

In the disarming of Queen's, Abercromby's scheme was shown to be practical if executed with discipline and if care was taken to avoid indiscriminate plundering. As successful was the disarming of parts of the South where Major-General John Moore (later to die a hero in the Peninsula) was sent to organize the campaign, which he did with restraint, decency – and considerable success.

In South Kildare, however, the free quarters were carried out with the reverse of Moore's restraint. From his headquarters at Athy, Colonel

Campbell of the 9th Dragoons let the army loose on the disturbed districts. The troops plundered indiscriminately, often threatening to burn down neighbourhoods. Before long the arms began to come in.

Paradoxically, it was on Thomas Reynolds that the full force of the free quarters campaign now fell. He was said to have made his newly restored castle, Kilkea (which he leased from the Fitzgerald family), an arms depot and headquarters for the Kildare rebels. Furthermore, Lord Edward himself was supposedly hidden deep inside. Late in April, Captain Erskine and troopers of the 9th Dragoons arrived and, with exemplary thoroughness, proceeded to gut Kilkea and destroy its contents. When, days later, they left disappointed, Kilkea was an empty shell. Nor was this an isolated incident.

It is clear that men like Campbell greatly outnumbered commanders like Moore. What had been seen so far, however, was the first phase of disarmament, executed less systematically and more brutally than Abercromby had proposed, but still recognizably his plan.

But despite the apparent success of the scheme, Camden had, after only a week, suddenly countermanded the free quarters throughout the distressed districts, ordering Lake instead to adopt 'other vigorous and effectual measures'. The real reason, of course, was the howl of rage from the gentry when they discovered that their own property might be injured, directly or indirectly. All they wanted was prompt punishment of the guilty. It was no time to observe the niceties of even martial law.

About 1 May, a large triangular construction of wooden scaffolding appeared in the main street of Athy. These 'triangles' were designed for securing a man while he was flogged with a cat-o'-nine-tails. Campbell had decided to use flogging not for punishment, but as an instrument of torture – to extort information about the concealed arms.

Although duly reported to the Government, the Castle made no effort to condemn these operations. With Lake's new phase, the recklessness of the Irish army would be given full rein.

Dublin and the South-East, 10–19 May

One of the United leaders from Kildare now played a decisive role in crushing the conspiracy – Thomas Reynolds. His ex-colleagues in the movement, convinced of his treachery, now had him reported to the Government as a United leader – whereupon Campbell threw him into Athy gaol. The same night a desperate plea reached his friend Cope. Reynolds, thoroughly appalled, was in no mood to refuse anything the Government asked.

In return for immunity he made a sworn statement about the underground army of Kildare and Lord Edward's role as general. Further, in exchange for a £5,000 lump sum and a life pension of £1,000, he agreed to appear as the principal witness in the treason trial of those arrested at Bond's.

For the Government, it was a triumph. News of the confession had already leaked out to the Kildare United committees, with excellent results. The organization was broken. Great numbers of pikes were being surrendered.

Edward Cooke was the man in charge of these matters. In early May, despite his informants, he was still largely ignorant of the plans of the main conspirators, or even of their identities. But now another Dublin barrister, Francis Magan, began to act secretly for the Castle.

Magan, one of first Catholics to be called to the Bar (the laws had been relaxed five years earlier), had, like Reynolds, been invited to join the revolutionary movement. With the disappearance of all but a handful of the original leaders, he now had a place on the Executive.

His first report startled even Cooke: the new Executive were planning a rising in about a fortnight. This conflicted with other information which stated that the rising was still timed to coincide with a French landing.

There now appeared a still more remarkable recruit for Cooke's intelligence service. On 10 May, a young militia captain named Armstrong was introduced by a fashionable Dublin bookseller to Henry Sheares. Armstrong promptly reported the interview, and was advised to act the part of the revolutionary. Within hours what purported to be the Executive's latest plans were on Cooke's desk.

Armstrong's information confirmed Magan's dramatically. The conspirators had decided not to wait for French aid, and would launch the general rising in the next few days. In the Dublin area it would take the form of a simultaneous night attack on the army camp at Loughlinstown, the barracks at Chapelizod, and the city itself.

In fact, the United movement's dilemma was no longer whether to fight now or wait for the French. It was whether to fight or surrender, for the Government's campaign had disastrously weakened the movement. Then, as disastrous, a coded message from the French declared that the expedition would not sail for four months.

Beset on all sides, the Executive now laid plans for a rising before the end of May. Districts were warned to prepare, and the other provinces told to co-ordinate their risings with the main one in

Dublin. Loughlinstown and Chapelizod would be handed over by their garrisons, and Dublin would fall, perhaps without a shot.

To succeed, this strategy depended above all on the attitude of the troops of the Dublin garrison. How far those regiments had been won over is hard to judge. But in truth, trusting to the garrison to join the cause was a desperate throw, which only the pitiable state of their affairs could justify.

Camden, now knowing that the United Executive planned to act within the next few days, needed no encouragement to order Lake to disarm the counties reported to be still ripe for revolution. The Government – like the county's gentry – had come to believe in Lake's 'prompt punishment' and 'salutary shocks'.

Dublin, 18–23 May

By the third week of May, the Government's forces engaged in the disarming were approaching Dublin itself. Only twelve miles to the west, the flames of burning houses lit the night sky.

In Dublin, however, society prepared to enjoy a great parliamentary spectacle. On Friday 18 May Robert, Earl of Kingston, was to be tried for the murder of his illegitimate half-brother, who had seduced his sixteen-year-old daughter. With its piquant mixture of mystery, scandal, and high society, it would be the trial of the century. He had elected to be tried by his peers – the first such trial

for forty years. But it proved an anti-climax, for no one came forward to prosecute, and each peer duly declared Kingston 'Not guilty upon mine honour'.

In fact, Kingston's trial nearly provided a theatrical climax beyond the wildest dreams of scandalmongers. The day before, the United Executive met in Dublin to discuss a scheme of breathtaking simplicity. At Kingston's trial next day would be virtually the entire Government of Ireland, from the Viceroy down. The United army needed only to surround the Houses of Parliament and seize the members of the Government, and the country would be theirs.

The plan was put to the ballot. The result was even until defeated by the vote of Francis Magan. Nothing shows better the state of the United movement than that their latest desperate scheme should have been defeated by a spy.

The Executive were divided as to the form the rising should take. On the 18th they met once more to try to resolve the split. Lawless and the Sheares brothers, adamant that it was too great a risk to let the country people march on Dublin, still pinned their hopes on the garrison coming over to them. Lord Edward and the rest insisted their only chance was to rally the combined armies of the four surrounding counties – Dublin, Meath, Kildare and Wicklow – and march in overwhelming strength on the capital. This plan was adopted, but at a high cost. The

BELOW: Reports of government atrocities in Ireland were often only too accurate. LEFT: Captain Swayne pitch-capping the people of Prosperous; CENTRE: half-hanging to get information; RIGHT: Hepenstall 'the walking gallows'. Engravings from the Irish Magazine *(1810).*

CAPᵀⁿ SWAYNE
Pitch Capping the People of Prosperous

PLAN of a TRAVELLING GALLOWS used in the YEAR 1798.

dedicated to the Ancient & Modern Britons, by their dutiful Servᵗ W. Cox

HEPENSTALL
'the walking Gallows'

Sheares brothers resigned, while Lawless threw up the whole enterprise and fled Ireland.

The rising was now agreed for 23 May. Lord Edward made hasty arrangements to co-ordinate the march of the four rebel armies. He himself would leave Dublin next evening – Saturday 19 May – to prepare a rallying point.

That evening he had an ominously close brush with Sirr and his men, but he managed to dodge back to a safe house in Thomas Street.

Next morning there was an anxious moment when a party of soldiers, led by Sirr, was spotted near by. Then the hunt seemed to be abandoned. Neilson called at lunchtime, and again at four, as usual taking no precaution to conceal himself.

And then, without warning, the blow fell. It was just seven when two men peered round the door of Lord Edward's room, one the Police Chief, Major Swan, the other a yeomanry officer, Captain Ryan. Lord Edward sprang up 'like a tiger' stabbing Swan three times in the side and chest.

Swan fired his pistol, missed, then ran downstairs, shouting, to fetch Sirr and his party of soldiers.

Now Ryan grappled with Lord Edward, the two of them rolling, locked together, down the stairs. Here Sirr at last came to the rescue of Ryan, still clinging to Lord Edward, though his stomach had been ripped open by fourteen stab wounds. 'I fired at Lord Edward's dagger arm,' Sirr later reported, 'and the instrument of death fell to the ground.' But Ryan's wounds were mortal. Lord Edward, only slightly wounded, it seemed, in one shoulder, was taken by the soldiers to the Castle.

Faced with this unexpected triumph, the Government arrested the other members of the Executive. Armstrong was instructed to arrange a last meeting with the Sheares brothers, and their arrest next morning, 21 May, seemed to complete the decapitation of the conspiracy – except for Neilson. Moreover, Sirr found a powerful weapon to turn against the rebels: a draft proclamation in John Sheares's handwriting which described the

'Whipping at Marlborough Green' where John Claudius Beresford, son of the Commissioner of Revenue and himself head of the merchant corps of yeomanry, used the cat-o'-nine-tails to get information. Another engraving of 1810.

brothers' plan for a rising within Dublin, but which was also a call to arms, a new statement of revolutionary ideals, a solemn cry for 'Vengeance, Irishmen, vengeance on your oppressors'.

There was now one essential counter-measure. On the morning of 22 May the city magistrates, assisted by 800 Dublin yeomanry, began disarming the city. Scenes that had become commonplace in the Midlands were now repeated in suspect areas of the capital. Houses were ransacked, buildings fired, and suspects dealt with in the usual way.

By the morning of 23 May, Camden, for one, felt unqualified relief. The great United Irish conspiracy had been severely damaged, and was now in its death throes. When the last districts had been disarmed, the campaign would be complete.

Then reports began to arrive that threw the Castle into the wildest confusion. A spy planted in one of Dublin's local committees arrived with the news that his troop had just been told to mobilize. Worse, Cooke learned that two deputies had been sent to raise Kildare and Wicklow. Further messages confirmed that the counties round Dublin were to rise that night and march on the city.

The Government had relied on Armstrong's account of the Sheareses' plan for a rising inside the city on Monday or Tuesday, confirmed by the actual draft proclamation seized by Sirr. But they believed that this had been frustrated by the trials, arrests and subsequent disarming of the city. What they had not known was that the Sheareses' plan, and indeed the brothers themselves, had been discarded before that fiery proclamation was drafted.

As the drum beat to arms in Dublin, people heard that immense bodies of rebels were actually assembling north and south of the city. Some of Dublin's loyalists seriously wondered if they should live to see another dawn. Incredibly, the Government had still not imposed a curfew, and crowds milled about the streets.

In fact there were few rebels to see. The Dublin arm of the movement had virtually disintegrated.

That night at about eight the Executive met despondently to try to co-ordinate Dublin's efforts with the main body of insurgents marching on the capital. Eventually Neilson volunteered to carry a message to the colonels of the few societies still intact. He then took himself to a pub. When he emerged, he staggered across to Newgate, shouting incoherently. A party of yeomanry was called, and a struggling Neilson was carried bodily inside.

Reports of his arrest spread rapidly. Telling their men to fend for themselves, the United leaders hastily dispersed.

RIGHT: On 19 May, Lord Edward Fitzgerald, the reputed commander-in-chief of the United Irish armies, stabbed to death Captain Ryan who was sent to arrest him, and was then shot and mortally wounded by Town Major Sirr. An 1845 engraving.

PART TWO REBEL

The storming of Prosperous barracks on the night of 23–4 May. Most of the garrison were piked or burnt to death. A loyalist view of the scene by George Cruikshank. (1845)

Dublin and surrounding counties 24–25 May

THE IDEA of stopping the mail coaches – as the signal for the rising beyond Dublin – was an ingenious one. The men detailed to halt them were stationed on the main roads not far from the city boundaries. Beyond, all along the county border in a broad crescent running from five to fifteen miles from the capital, parties of armed rebels, perhaps 10,000 in all, now began to take up their positions.

They were not, however, an organized force. Unhappily, faith in French assistance had blinded most of the Executive to the real nature of the war ahead; the county committees had no instructions as to how to structure, train and command an army; and in the event, people were expected to fend for themselves – ill-armed, untrained, and without concerted plans. Moreover, most of the local commanders were men of little education and military understanding.

In the strategic county of Kildare, however, there were commanders of exceptional enterprise.

LION

ABOVE: Kildare rebels piking an old man, George Crawford, and his granddaughter. Another scene from Cruikshank (1845) based on loyalist accounts.

Their leader was a respectable Catholic landholder from Johnstown, Michael Reynolds. At his side was another Catholic, even more respectable, Dr John Esmonde of Sallins. Furthermore, as yeomanry officers, Reynolds, Esmonde and most of the other Kildare leaders had received some formal military training. These men now adopted a simple, desperate scheme for capturing Naas and the neighbouring garrisons.

The Government believed that Lake, through his commanders like Campbell, had broken the conspiracy in Kildare. The spirit of rebellion seemed crushed.

And then, on 23 May, an express galloped into the headquarters of the District Commander, Lieutenant-General Sir Ralph Dundas, near Kilcullen: a rising was expected at any moment in Dublin and the adjacent districts. At once the garrisons were alerted. But it was now nearly midnight and no warning could be given before morning to the dozens of other detachments scattered across the county.

One such party was at Prosperous, a small town to the north of Naas. Here there were some two dozen Welsh Fencibles – regiments raised in the war – and thirty-five of the City of Cork militia under a zealous Protestant, Captain Swayne.

Three miles to the east, at the small village of Clane, there were fifty men of the Armagh militia. They had the Clane yeomanry in support, though only twenty of them were on duty. There had been no hint of danger of any sort.

It was now a few hours from dawn on 24 May, and in the area around Dublin the great insurrection to liberate Ireland seemed to be degenerating into a few scattered risings by leaderless men. At the Naul, near the northern end of the crescent of rebels, at Dunboyne to the west, and at Rathfarnham near Clondalkin to the south, small local successes soon dissolved into fiasco, the insurgents proving to be little more than marauding bands reminiscent of the Defenders, and quick to melt away at any sign of organized resistance. An engagement near Clondalkin between the 5th Dragoons and the few remaining rebels of the area's original 500 or so, resulted in the Dragoons sending a wagonload of pikes and three mangled bodies to Dublin.

To cap it all, the mail coach signal had completely miscarried. Only one of the five coaches was stopped in the appointed place, at Santry, three miles to the north of Dublin. The rebels fired it – to no effect, for on the strategic road to Belfast, no one stirred.

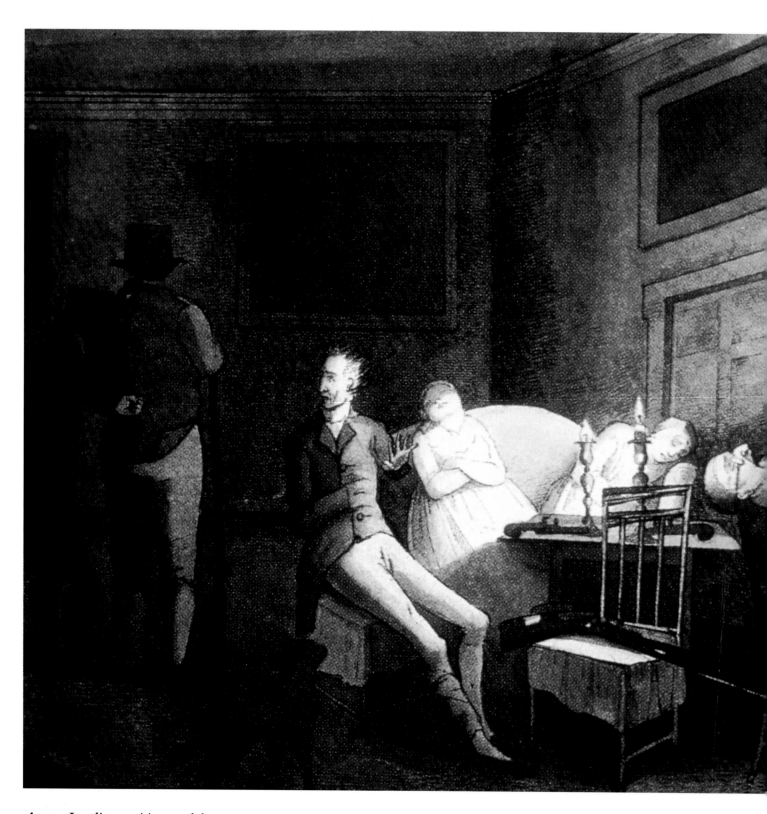

ABOVE: Loyalists awaiting attack by the rebels on a country house in Wicklow. A contemporary watercolour by an eye-witness, Caroline Hamilton, showing how war is an odd mixture of terror and boredom.

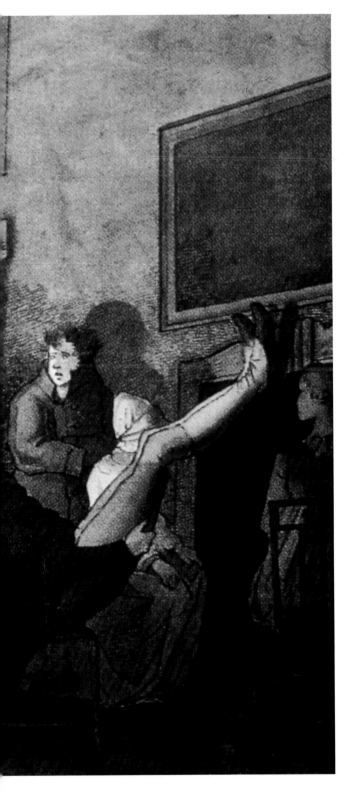

At about three in the morning more than 300 rebels attacked Clane, killing several of the Armagh militia in their billets. The yeomanry managed to beat off the attack while the militia turned out, and then both forces drove the attackers beyond the village. Many rebels were killed; six were captured and executed out of hand.

Returning to Clane, they received grim news. At Prosperous, Swayne and his little garrison had been surprised by a great mob of rebels, commanded by the yeomanry's own first lieutenant, Esmonde. Most of the troops, including Swayne, had been butchered. The commander of the yeomanry was Richard Griffith, a liberal Protestant landlord. He hardly had time to regroup his force before a wave of attackers swept down on Clane along the road from Prosperous. Disciplined fire killed many rebels, and a charge by Griffith and his yeomanry put them to flight, throwing away their weapons and their looted equipment as they ran.

Griffith was now ordered to retire on Naas. As they made ready, a yeoman called Mite confessed that he had actually accompanied Esmonde for the attack on Prosperous, but had not taken part in the action. Just then Esmonde himself appeared and took his usual place at the right of the troop. Griffith, speechless with astonishment and indignation, rode beside him into Naas, where he was immediately gaoled.

Meanwhile, Reynolds had launched a full-scale attack on the large and well-armed garrison

ABOVE: 'The Irish rebel who threatened to murder Mrs Tighe.' A contemporary sketch by Maria Spilsbury.

United Irishmen in Training.

RIGHT: 'United Irishmen in Training'. Gillray's caricature, published in 1798, based on reports in London newspapers. Note the inn sign: the Tree of Liberty.

at Naas. The rebels advanced against the gaol and the barracks in two columns. Time and again they charged, fighting with demented courage against the militia's cannon. But at last they broke, fleeing in every direction. Now the cavalry were let loose on them, turning defeat into massacre. Abandoned pikes and mangled rebel corpses – some 300 in all – littered the streets and fields for miles. The garrison lost twenty-two men – and Reynolds escaped.

It was the job of General Dundas to crush the insurrection before it spread. He could not organize his counter-attack, however, for rebel pikemen had occupied a strong position at Old Kilcullen, close to his headquarters. Dundas had only sixty troops at his disposal, and two-thirds of them were cavalry, whose short swords made them practically useless against the pikemen. Nevertheless, they eagerly galloped away to charge the rebel position.

The result was inevitable – thrown back three times, twenty-three officers and men were killed, and ten wounded.

Dundas cut his way out, and fell back on Kilcullen Bridge, where he was able to collect together the local yeomanry, about a hundred in all. Meanwhile the rebels had positioned themselves astride his line of retreat to the north, their numbers swelled by their success.

This time Dundas did not underestimate his opponents. Feinting against their flanks, he drew them into the fire of his musketeers, then cut them to pieces with cavalry. The troops were in no mood to give quarter: 'About 150 lay dead – no prisoners.' His force suffered no casualties.

It was now nearly twenty-four hours since the first rebel parties had assembled for the assault on Dublin. Fourteen engagements had followed, and in all but two even the most meagre garrison had managed to repulse the rebels. In short, there was much reason to think that the rebellion would swiftly collapse.

But now Dundas, far from driving home his advantage, gave the order for a general retirement on Naas. Obediently, the garrisons, including the yeomanry, of Clane, Ballitore, Monasterevin (though here the yeomanry stayed), even Kildare, all moved out. Only Athy retained its regular garrison, the messenger with the order to retreat having been killed by the rebels.

By nightfall, about 2,000 rebels occupied the town of Kildare. They took over the houses of the

United Irishmen upon Duty.

LEFT: 'United Irishmen upon Duty.' Another Gillray caricature of 1798.

loyalists who had fled, and seized and plundered the mail coach from Limerick, killing a young officer who was a passenger in it. Then, after murdering some of the Protestant loyalists, they marched out again, bent on attacking Monasterevin.

Dublin and surrounding counties; London, 25–27 May

Though the situation in Kildare was perilous, Dublin remained singularly undisturbed. Mild sensation was caused by the hanging, from a lamppost in the Castle yard, of two yeomen deserters captured at Clondalkin, and later by the dispatch of Dr Esmonde from the same makeshift gallows. A belated curfew was imposed, and all householders who had not registered their arms were ordered to surrender them forthwith.

Public response to the restrictions was heartening. But Camden saw beneath the loyalty of what he called the 'respectable' classes an ominous spirit of retaliation, perhaps no less destructive than the United movement itself. And every hour brought fresh accounts of looting and lynching by the infuriated Catholic peasantry who had borne the brunt of Lake's disarming.

By 25 May, with news of fresh disasters in Meath and Kildare, Camden began to feel seriously alarmed. He now urged on Portland and Pitt the 'absolute necessity' of sending reinforcements from Britain.

On the day the rebellion broke out, Pitt and the British cabinet were, for once, considering the Irish problem. The subject of their deliberations, however, was not tragedy, but farce.

A few months earlier five men had been arrested in the most peculiar circumstances at a hotel in Margate. One of these was Arthur O'Connor.

The legal case against O'Connor seemed solid enough, for it turned on highly incriminating documents found in his possession. Even so, the Irish Government, for whom O'Connor's conviction was of supreme importance, took no chances. Every effort was made to weaken or discredit the defence.

Yet at his trial at Maidstone on 21 May O'Connor outmanoeuvred everyone. The heart of his defence was a dazzling series of testimonials from the great English Whiggery, including Fox and Sheridan. Portrayed by the defence as a persecuted patriot, he was triumphantly acquitted.

The trial ended, however, in fiasco. O'Connor could be retried under Irish law on the same charge of which he had just been acquitted under English. Accordingly, two Bow Street runners were waiting by the dock to rearrest him. Suddenly O'Connor attempted to escape. In the ensuing fracas he nearly got away, but at the last minute was brought crashing to the floor.

When the news of the bungled trial, and the unseemly brawl that followed, reached the British cabinet, Pitt was in a sensitive mood. Intelligence showed that some sort of invasion attempt by the French was imminent.

Two days later, on 25 May, Pitt and the cabinet received from Ireland news they had long dreaded: the rebellion had begun.

In Ireland, Dundas's hasty withdrawal had opened all Kildare to the rebels. By 26 May an army of about 30,000 United men had occupied Kildare, Prosperous and Kilcullen, as well as Rathangan, Newbridge and Ballitore. Unless they could be forced on to the defensive, they would soon break out of the county.

The rebels were clearly massing for a thrust. At Monasterevin and Portarlington the garrisons had succeeded in driving the rebels off, killing many, but more attacks were expected. Desperate appeals for help were sent to the Government.

A still more dangerous situation existed on the county's north-eastern border. Attacks had been made on the 25th against Kilcock, Leixlip and Lucan. All three had been beaten off at severe cost to the rebels, yet they were still on the offensive, and were certain to attack again. Already Kildare men were pushing out northwards to link up with the thousands of United men still unsubdued in County Meath.

So far there had been no outbreak in the north of the county, around the border with King's. But on the 26th a party, described as 'five thousand Defenders', had taken Rathangan, killing most of the yeomanry garrison. They had then, without provocation, murdered nineteen Protestant men known or believed to be loyal to the Government. As before, the Catholic loyalists were left unharmed.

Even now, however, the rebellion might have died a natural death, but for two horrible tragedies.

On the morning of 24 May, the insurrection had spread south along the Dublin–Cork turnpike, engulfing the towns and villages at either side. As well as the towns captured in Kildare, all of the garrisons in Wicklow had had to beat

off attacks. To the south, Carlow was also heavily attacked on the 25th, as was Hacketstown. In both cases the rebels were driven off with heavy casualties, but they were still on the offensive.

To these bare details of rebel attacks were added wild stories of murder and treachery. Now, in their rage and panic, the loyalists took the law into their own hands. At Dunlavin the small garrison dragged twenty-eight prisoners from the gaol and executed them – men who had taken no part in the risings. Then, at Carnew, though the rebellion had not yet reached that area, twenty-eight suspects were marched out of the town prison and shot by yeomen and militia.

On 27 May, the day after the shootings at Carnew, news reached Dublin of a disaster of completely new dimensions. The insurrection had burst out in County Wexford in great force and was spreading south with terrifying rapidity.

Wexford, 23–29 May

In the centre and south of County Wexford, both the United movement and its adversaries were relatively inactive. The proclaiming of the whole county as a disturbed area at the end of April seemed, to the Government, to have brought the people to their senses. Yet counter-measures there were relatively light. By 23 May the magistrates were confident that by their mild measures they had weathered the storm.

In fact, others, better informed, had warned the Government that while the county appeared to be quiet, the movement was both strong and on the increase. It had derived unusual prestige and encouragement from three members of the landed gentry. The most important was Protestant – Bagenal Harvey of Bargay Castle. Two were Catholic – a young squire, Edward Fitzgerald of New Park, and a doctor, John Colclough of Ballyteigue. How far they really accepted the aims of their fellow revolutionaries it is difficult to know. Harvey, a popular and well-off landlord, certainly seems to have been, philosophically speaking, a republican. Certainly they themselves played no active part in organizing the county.

It was an entirely different story in the north-west of Wexford. Here outrages had been common since the previous autumn. Loyalists felt threatened on all sides, and were neither supported nor disciplined by a regular garrison.

On their part, the leaders of the United movement in northern Wexford, weak and hesitant themselves, launched a reckless propaganda

RIGHT: 'Erin Go Brach!' ('Ireland for ever!') James Gillray's caricature of an Irish rebel, often erroneously said to be Grattan, published in London in 1798.

Portrait of an Irish Chief; drawn from Life at Wexford.

campaign in an effort to establish control over the movement's supporters.

Reports began to circulate that the Orangemen were planning a massacre of the entire Catholic population. The story, strange enough in a place where Catholics outnumbered Protestants by thirty to one, was doubly absurd in Wexford, where there were virtually no Orangemen at all. But the people were prepared to believe it. Only the spark was now lacking to ignite them in an uncontrollable explosion.

On Sunday 20 May, the magistrates on the Wexford–Wicklow border began a campaign of terror. As the flogging and burning spread through the district, they pressed home their advantage. By the end of that week the United organization there appeared to be disintegrating.

The next area to be cleared was the eastern frontier land adjoining Arklow, where little progress had been made against the conspiracy. Then one of the Arklow leaders confessed and gave the names of his associates. One of these, Anthony Perry, a Protestant, was arrested on 23 May and tortured with a 'pitch-cap' – in which pitch was rubbed on the victim's head, gunpowder added and the mixture then set alight. Perry confessed, naming twenty-two members of the United party – including Harvey and Fitzgerald.

But also seeping southwards to central Wexford was a wave of hysteria fed by tales of atrocity, some of them only too true, some circulated by reckless members of the United party. By the night of Friday 25 May it reached a crescendo. Whole villages were emptied as people fled the murderous Orangemen.

In general, the Catholic priests retained some authority over the peasantry, disabusing them of foolish stories of massacre. The exceptions were the curates of two villages which the yeomanry were now disarming; Father John Murphy of Boulavogue and Father Michael Murphy of Ballycanew. For days they had heard the tales of torture and massacre. Now the yeomanry had arrived, and were acting as expected of them.

Then came the news of the atrocities at Dunlavin and Carnew. It seemed there was now an *official* policy of extermination. Almost immediately followed wild rumours of rebel successes in County Kildare. Faced with tales of Government massacres and United triumphs, the insurgents could restrain themselves no longer. Though Father Michael wavered, Father John agreed to lead the campaign of resistance.

RIGHT: Father Murphy, the United Irish leader in Wexford, showing his flock what he thought of heretic bullets. Another Cruikshank illustration (1845) based on loyalist accounts.

ABOVE: Wexford rebels helping themselves at the table of the Bishop of Ferns. By Cruikshank (1845).

About eight o'clock that evening, Father John's men attacked a patrol from the Camolin yeomanry, killing the two officers.

By the afternoon of the following day, Whit Sunday, Father John's party established themselves on Oulart Hill, having first raided the countryside for arms – and having murdered a number of Protestants and fired their houses. But despite the arms they had seized, they were still exceedingly ill equipped to meet regular troops, or even the vengeful yeomanry.

In the town of Wexford people knew nothing of these events – except the alarming discovery from Perry's confession that Fitzgerald and Harvey were United leaders. Harvey was arrested and put in the town gaol; and during the night Fitzgerald and Colclough were also brought in.

On the morning of Whit Sunday came news of the rising at Oulart – only twenty miles to the north. Rumours exaggerated the danger, but most people remained calm. Wexford was a walled town, easy to defend, and the garrison comprised a strong detachment of the North Cork militia, with additional yeomanry, under

Colonel Foote, a veteran of the American war. In due course the militia, eager to get to grips with the 'banditti', marched out towards Oulart. At about mid-afternoon they breasted a ridge to find Father John's pikemen drawn up in a commanding position on Oulart Hill.

Colonel Foote, meanwhile, was struggling to restrain his men. His own view was that he was too weak to attack the rebels – uphill, heavily outnumbered, and with inexperienced troops (his men were raw recruits, mostly Catholics) unsupported by artillery. Such defeatism was too much for the Irish gentlemen in his command, however, and for their men, many of whom were still warm with drink they had looted from a pub along the way. For a moment Foote's back was turned, as he wrote a message for reinforcements. Then he looked up, and saw a terrible sight.

Without permission, the second-in-command had given the order to charge. In vain Foote tried to recall them as they surged up the stony hillside. Then his command – 109 officers and men – was swallowed up.

The carnage was so sudden and so complete that few of the soldiers even tried to escape. They were rounded up one by one by the peasants, though they waved their missals and cried out they 'were Catholics too'. No quarter was given them, or to the wounded.

Two hours later, Colonel Foote, a sergeant and two privates rode back into Wexford. They were the sole survivors of all that force.

The immediate threat was now to the large garrison town of Enniscorthy. Nearby a second rising had taken place that morning, led by the other Father Murphy, Father Michael. They had been dispersed by the local corps of yeomanry, and the remnants now joined the main body from Oulart.

Early on Whit Monday, Father John's army marched into Ferns, abandoned by its garrison the previous day. The hungry rebels poured through the town, gutting the houses of people that they considered Orangemen, including the elegant palace of Dr Eusebius Cleaver, the Protestant bishop, which they sacked and left a smoking ruin.

By that same morning the commander of the garrison at Enniscorthy, Captain Snowe, had organized the defence, stationing his best troops at two of the town's main entrances, and the rest at strongpoints in the centre. His total force was comparatively large: 80 militia, 200 local yeomanry, and a number of civilian volunteers – in all, perhaps 400 effectives. The problem lay in disposing them against a force of thousands.

At about one o'clock the outposts galloped in with the news that the rebels were advancing in one immense body on the Duffrey Gate.

Dublin and surrounding counties, 26–29 May

By 26 May, all Kildare except the border towns had been abandoned to the United army. The Government had thus lost control of the strategic roads to Cork and Limerick. They had also allowed a large force of rebels to blockade a third strategic road, running to the north-west by way of County Meath.

The United army in Meath was posted astride the Navan road a few miles to the north of

ABOVE: Rebels dancing the Carmagnolle in a captured house. By Cruikshank (1845).

Dunshaughlin. Their camp was on the summit of a hill – on Tara, indeed, the seat of the High Kings of Ireland. More important still, its walls and banks afforded good protection from fire.

The local yeomanry had watched helplessly as the rebels plundered the countryside. At about six o'clock in the evening of the 26th, however, three companies of Scotch Fencibles appeared. Their commander, Captain Blanche, with a total of 300 Fencibles and yeomanry and a 6-pounder gun, led them up towards the enemy's stronghold. The place seemed black with rebels; but by nightfall, defeated by superior discipline and musketry, as well as the 6-pounder's grapeshot, they had been driven off Tara in disorder. Some 350 rebels were killed; Blanche's losses were 13 dead and 28 wounded.

The strategic benefits were huge. The rebels in Meath and the North Midlands were completely dispersed; a firebreak between North and South created; the road to the North reopened; and one threat to the capital removed. That all this could be achieved by so small a force was not lost on the Government's detractors.

By his precipitate retreat, Dundas had proved himself unsuited to the military task. He did, however, recognize that most of the Kildare rebels had been caught up in the rising by accident, and that few were guilty of atrocities. In short, he was ready to impose a surrender in Kildare on generous terms.

The Kildare rebels had four strategic camps. From one of these, Knockallen Hill, a deputation now reached Dundas, offering surrender in exchange for complete pardon. His civil reply encouraged the rebels to try to improve on these terms, which in turn prompted Camden to order that their 'arrogant' offer be refused point blank. But Dundas had already agreed more generous terms. The next day, on 29 May, he accepted the surrender of 3,000 men, assuring them of protection. Having given up their arms, leaders and all were allowed to disperse to their homes.

Dundas now started to arrange a similar surrender of one of the remaining three camps, a larger one on the Curragh. But before anything could be concluded, an appalling tragedy destroyed all hopes of a quick end to the rebellion in the Midlands.

For six days now all Munster and other parts of the south-west had been cut off from the capital. Even when reports of the rising finally arrived, the various local commanders proved incapable of concerted action. On Sunday, how-ever, the Limerick commander, General Sir James Duff, had decided to act on his own. He organized a flying column which by forced marches covered the hundred-odd miles in forty-eight hours. On Tuesday morning, 29 May, they galloped into the smoking ruins of Kildare. Determined to 'make a dreadful example of the rebels', they marched grimly on to the rebel camp on the Curragh.

Unknown to Duff, the Curragh rebels had assembled at a prehistoric fort called Gibbet Rath to make terms with Dundas. A few minutes more and it would have been completed. But just at that moment, and despite a warning from Dundas to Duff, the rebels found the latter's vengeful army advancing upon their rear.

Several thousand people, many unarmed, were now set upon by an infuriated pack of militia and dragoons. Three hundred and fifty were cut down.

Elsewhere in the Midlands similar clashes brought equally disastrous consequences.

On Saturday the garrison commander at Athy, the notorious Colonel Campbell, received an offer of unconditional surrender from the people of Ballitore. He replied that he would accept the offer, provided all their arms were deposited on a nearby hill by six o'clock that evening.

In Ballitore, however, the rebels now equivocated, but eventually they made a new offer: they would send six respectable men as hostages. It was nearly midnight before they received Campbell's reply: the hostages must be sent before morning; otherwise the army would show the rebels no mercy.

And now a completely new danger emerged. Troops from Carlow, knowing nothing of these arrangements, arrived on the outskirts in the early hours of Whit Sunday. In the ensuing panic, 'the people fled and dispersed', so that the hostages could not be gathered.

When the coming surrender was explained, the soldiers turned back, but by now Campbell's ultimatum had expired. He decided to make an example of Ballitore. Hardly had the Carlow troops marched out than the Athy troops moved in, bent on punishment and revenge.

The majority of the inhabitants were assumed to be guilty. Many of them were shot or hacked to death. Most of the houses were burnt to the ground; and those left standing were stripped and looted.

The real rebels were still a force to be reckoned with. At Rathangan they defeated a squadron of dragoons sent to drive them from the town. A couple of hours later, however, a substantial body of militia sent the rebels flying in confusion. A cavalry charge completed the rout, and about fifty or sixty people were shot or sabred. No prisoners were taken.

As crude and confused as actions such as those at Ballitore and Rathangan were, the counter-attack in the Midlands did seem to be achieving its immediate object: to defeat the rebels and restore the Government's control.

But all over Kildare and Wicklow there lurked the remnants of the armies they had beaten. As fugitives and outlaws, they still represented a grave threat to the Government.

And now a new threat materialized. On 30 May, news arrived that confirmed Camden's worst fears. Not only was Ulster, which had all this time remained quiet, still organized: its Executive had just met to co-ordinate plans for general rebellion.

Ulster and Leinster, 29 May–8 June

The news that the North was about to rise had come from another important Castle spy, Nicholas Magin, a young Catholic who had penetrated to the Ulster provincial Executive.

His report of an imminent rising was all the more shocking because, until recently, the southern rising had not apparently shaken the inertia of the northern United leaders. Then, at a meeting on Tuesday 29 May, the mood had suddenly changed. The Ulster Executive had been denounced and voted out of office for failing to carry out Ulster's part in the agreed national plan for a rising. They were replaced by younger and more violent men. These now planned for Down and Antrim, the two counties that were the closest to Belfast, and the best armed and organized, to act as the trigger for the Ulster rising.

The new Executive was led by a friend of Tone's, Henry Joy McCracken, a prosperous cotton manufacturer. Young as he was, he had been a member of the United movement since the days when Belfast had been its centre.

By 6 June, he had rallied to his standard perhaps 12,000 Antrim men in all. As many again were expected from County Down, and about half that number from Tyrone and Armagh. The rising would commence next morning with a combined attack on Antrim, the strategic centre of Ulster.

In County Wexford, meanwhile, Enniscorthy had fallen to the rebels. For the soldiers, the odds had been impossible. By mid-afternoon Snowe had lost over a hundred men, and half Enniscorthy was on fire. Several costly charges dislodged the enemy for a time, but Snowe knew they had won only a breathing space. At four o'clock he had the retreat sounded, and the survivors staggered back along the Wexford road, the only way still open to them.

Despite this disaster, and the unnerving sight of the Enniscorthy refugees pouring in, the Wexford garrison did not despair. Their weak forces had been reinforced, and now numbered over 1,000, including several hundred civilian volunteers. Still more encouraging was news that General Fawcett was marching to their relief with a contingent of regulars and two howitzers.

Unfortunately, and unknown to the people of Wexford, the party with the howitzers – seventy militia and eighteen gunners – somehow over-took Fawcett. As they reached an outcrop known as the Three Rocks, about four miles from the town, a wave of pikemen engulfed the column. Almost all were shot or hacked to death.

The disaster was followed by another, with even more serious results. At first light on Wednesday the Wexford garrison commander, Lieutenant-Colonel Jonas Watson, led a force out towards Three Rocks to link up with the expected relief column. Although they avoided the ambush, Watson himself fell in the encounter. His death brought consternation to the garrison, which turned to despair when it was learned that Fawcett, now believing the rebels too strong to risk an engagement, had withdrawn.

The new garrison commander still resisted evacuation. But panic prevailed. Along the road westwards some yeomanry were in full flight. Other troops followed, their retreat marked by a trail of burning buildings, and the bodies of people shot as they worked the fields. The towns-people were left to fend for themselves.

Wexford was now completely at the mercy of the rebel force, whose discipline was no better than that of the army they had beaten. The streets were soon choked with men firing random shots. By and large, the women and children were not molested. Any man, however, suspected of dis-loyalty to the new regime was immediately imprisoned – which meant, in practice, most of the Protestant men of all classes.

Meanwhile a second relief column was at last

marching on Wexford, on the direct orders of the Castle. By the 29th, Lake had sent 250 men under General Loftus to drive southwards into Wicklow. He had then reinforced them with 400 men under Camden's friend and personal aide, Colonel Walpole, a young courtier whose only qualification seems to have been a desire to prove himself in battle. Lake now ordered these forces to march on into Wexford.

There were two other detachments also moving southwards, one at Newtownbarry and the other at Carnew. Loftus ordered both to help him encircle the advance guard of the rebels at Ballymore Hill, which threatened the garrison at Gorey. Walpole was given firm orders that whatever his position at the Castle, he must obey his military superior.

Loftus now divided his force: from Gorey he would take the coast road to Ballymore, Walpole taking a short cut inland, with orders to stay in line with Loftus and to send word if he encountered the enemy. The Newtownbarry and Carnew detachments would also march on Ballymore.

The two columns left Gorey on the morning of 4 June. Despite misgivings, Loftus had had to entrust Walpole with twice his own force and three all-important cannon.

Six hours later, an officer galloped into Dublin with grim news for the Viceroy. Walpole had been ambushed. He and most of his men had been killed or wounded. The survivors (including Captain Armstrong, wounded) had fled back into Wicklow. Loftus had abandoned Gorey and retreated far to the north.

In defiance of Loftus's orders, and against his own officers' advice, Walpole had pushed on towards the rebel position. Where the road ran between high banks crowned with thick hedges, his column had, in a few moments, been overwhelmed by a wave of infuriated rebels. Most of their arms and equipment, and all three guns, were lost to the enemy. Worst of all, the disaster gave the rebels back the initiative on a broad strategic front.

It was now that the Castle, reeling and fearful, received the long-dreaded message from General Nugent in Belfast. The North had risen.

Even this, however, was nothing to the chilling news that just then arrived from London. Bonaparte's intentions had at last become clear. He had sailed with a fleet from Toulon on the 19th. His destination was understood to be Ireland.

ABOVE: Cruikshank's grim picture of the scene at Scullabogue barn, Country Wexford on June 5. About 200 men, women and children, almost all Protestant, were piked or burnt to death by United Irishmen. The massacre sent shock waves around Ireland, alienating many Northern Presbyterians who had previously supported the movement (1845).

The Battle of Arklow on 9 June, the turning point of the Wexford rising. An army of Wexford rebels, led by Father Murphy and reputed 19,000 strong, stormed the Wicklow border town 'like madmen' and were flung back with huge losses. An engraving by an unknown loyalist published in 1799.

PART THREE REVOL

Wexford, 30 May–5 June

*I*N WEXFORD, the first night of the Irish Republic passed in comparative calm. Next day, however, the need for some form of leadership dawned upon the people. Two Catholic gentlemen – Colclough and Fitzgerald – were appointed colonels. As for Harvey, despite the fact that he was a Protestant and a landlord, he had been the inspiration of the United movement in Wexford, and the people rushed to release him, then appointed him Commander-in-Chief. These three began the daunting task of imposing some sort of order on the lawless army.

Their immediate task was to try to prevent further outrages. A retired British officer, Captain Matthew Keogh, was made military governor, responsible for protecting the town. Harvey and the other leaders also formed a kind of committee of public safety, which put a stop to indiscriminate plunder and introduced a system of food rationing.

The second task – to protect the loyalists – proved harder. Many rebels had excellent reasons to hate anyone connected with the Government, feelings exacerbated by the tales of Orange atrocities spread by United agents. Now an influential party among the rebels was bent on retaliation.

One measure taken to safeguard the town paid an unexpectedly swift dividend. Commandeered

UTION

Henry Joy McCracken's United Irish seal (LEFT) and twentieth century portrait (RIGHT). As commander of the United army of Antrim he was one of the few original political leaders of the movement to take part in a battle.

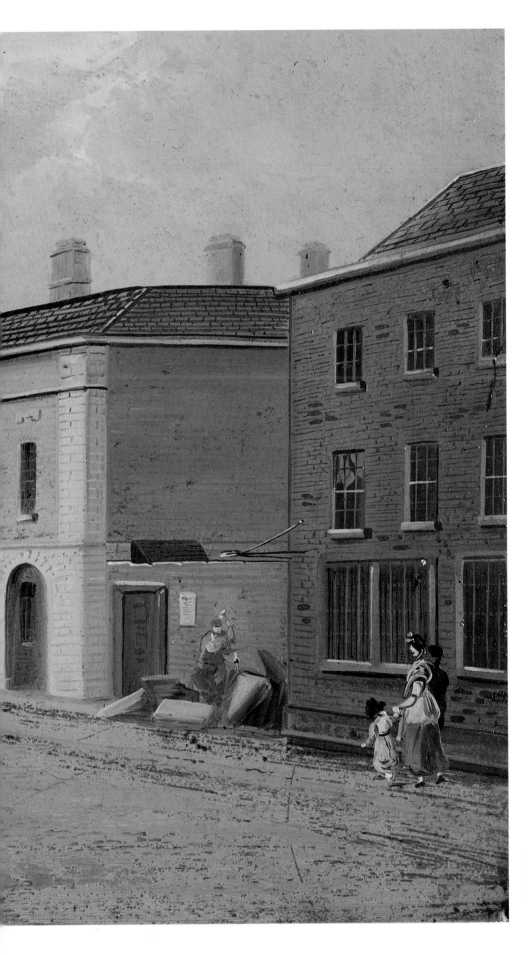

LEFT: *Belfast Assembly Rooms (upper storey, above arches), where McCracken was tried and condemned to be hanged.*

oyster boats had been sent to patrol the bay, and these now intercepted a number of coasters carrying provisions. A more flamboyant prize came with the capture of Lord Kingsborough, who was on his way to rejoin his regiment at Wexford, unaware that the town was in rebel hands.

It was now 3 June, the fourth day of the rebel occupation. For the prisoners, hopes of release were being replaced by fear of murder. In desperation, many Protestants begged to be received into the Catholic Church.

Meanwhile, Harvey had left Wexford for the rebel camp at Three Rocks, where he assumed command of the main republican army. He was not the man to lead them. He had no military experience, no real fellow feeling with the people, no burning revolutionary fervour. On the contrary, he seemed sickened by the turn of events.

Precious days had been lost while the leaders tried to impose some sort of order. At length about half their forces had been sent north in two contingents; one, under Perry and Fitzgerald, to the Wicklow border, the other, under a local priest, Father Kearns, to Newtownbarry. Harvey was to lead the third and largest contingent against New Ross. Despite the time lost, he had every prospect of success.

Reaching Carrickbyrne Hill, his army wasted two more days. At last they got moving again. On the night of 4 June they made camp at Corbet Hill, overlooking New Ross. That night Harvey drew up a rough battle plan for a simultaneous attack on three sides of the town.

In New Ross, Major-General Henry Johnson had done his best to exploit the time the rebels' delays had brought him. He decided that the main attack would come from the east, directly below the enemy's camp. Despite the difficulty of defending the town, he was fairly confident: disciplined troops, properly led and supported by artillery, would always defeat an irregular force, however large. That evening a sizeable contingent of the Dublin militia under their colonel, Lord Mountjoy (formerly Luke Gardiner), marched into the town. They brought the garrison's strength to more than 2,000 and, crucially, raised the number of cannon to six.

Johnson set his forward position outside the Three Bullet Gate, directly below the rebel camp. Here he placed a battalion of regulars and militia with two guns. Outside the Bishop's Gate he formed a second defensive position. Within the town the rest of the infantry and artillery were established around a series of strongpoints and

at the vital wooden bridge across the Barrow at their backs.

It was now just before dawn on Tuesday 5 June. In the half light, a rebel horseman galloped down towards the Three Bullet Gate. The sentries took no chances, and the rider fell. It was Harvey's aide; in his pocket was a message urging the garrison to surrender or face destruction.

A few minutes later a mass of rebels swept down from Corbet Hill and threw themselves against the defences at the Three Bullet Gate.

Meanwhile, a ghastly scene was being enacted near by.

At Scullabogue, near Carrickbyrne, the rebels had established a makeshift gaol in an empty house and adjoining barn. The majority of the loyalist prisoners – nearly two hundred, including women and children – were Protestant. Soon after the first attack on New Ross, a messenger arrived with orders to kill the prisoners in retaliation for atrocities committed by the soldiers. The rebel captain in charge refused. Another order came, and was again refused, and then a third. The guards could no longer be restrained.

One group dragged the prisoners from the house and shot them four at a time on the lawn. Other rebels fired the barn's thatch. The terrified families inside twice succeeded in opening the heavy door, but were thrust back by pikes. At last the screams faded into silence. In the ruins, charred bodies were found still standing upright for want of space.

The guards spent several days turning over the corpses for coins or other valuables.

New Ross and North Wexford, 5–8 June
At about seven the same morning, General Johnson, superintending the defence of the Three Bullet Gate, saw something incredible taking place. Inch by inch, the defences were being battered down. Quite suddenly, the line gave way, and several hundred attackers swept through the gate and charged on into the town. There was not a moment to lose. Johnson sent McCormick, his aide, for reinforcements to seal the defences.

The United leaders had been taken equally by surprise. Harvey had sent a popular young man called John Kelly with 800 men to drive in the outposts. They had strict instructions not to attack the town itself, but to hold off until the other two divisions of the army were in position.

Whether Kelly ignored his orders, or whether he could not restrain his men, burning to avenge the shooting of the envoy, they took the gate and swept on, another company following them.

Kelly was badly wounded, but his men now split into two columns. One vanished into the smoke, while the other charged downhill and on towards the strongpoint on the Main Guard. Here they were cut down by grapeshot. After a confused struggle the survivors regained the edge of the town.

Meanwhile the other two divisions of Harvey's army had been disconcerted by Kelly's pre-emptive attack. In the general confusion some of their men joined the central body, but the majority panicked and fled. The huge army of 20,000 was now reduced by half.

The day would by now have been Johnson's, but for one fatal blunder.

He had planned to keep his small force of cavalry in reserve, knowing that they were useless against determined pikemen. But some dragoons were now ordered – by whom, no one knows – to support the defence at the Three Bullet Gate. As they rode out the pikemen turned, and in a few minutes the commanding officer and twenty-eight dragoons lay dead.

To complete the disaster, Lord Mountjoy had for some reason ridden out towards the rebel lines; possibly he was trying to persuade the people to surrender. Struck down, he lay wounded by the gate until finished off by a pikeman.

The effect upon the United army's morale was immediate. Cheering wildly, they returned to the attack. Again the defenders were rolled back through the Three Bullet Gate.

Confusion followed. Soldiers and civilians ran towards the bridge, pursued by yelling rebels. Flames rose from cabins opposite the churchyard, leaping from roof to roof. The rebels were driving deeper into the town, the battle's centre now apparently Main Guard.

Thrown back at the first assault, the pikemen ran down the narrow streets, firing the thatch. Soon half the town was burning. But still they could not take Main Guard, where two guns swept the vital crossroads guarding the approach to the bridge.

Apart from Main Guard, and a strongpoint manned by the Clare militia at the Market Gate, only Johnson's own position near the Three Bullet Gate still held out. McCormick was again sent back to find reinforcements. But no one he met was prepared to join the general.

Desperate, Johnson galloped off to fetch help himself. He found a stream of soldiers pouring back across the bridge. Still worse, some earlier fugitives had turned back a large contingent of militia marching to the relief of the town.

It was now about midday. In Johnson's absence, resistance at the Three Bullet Gate had collapsed within minutes. Except for a dozen men with the guns at the Main Guard, an old loyalist with seven men near by, and the militia at the Market Gate, New Ross had been abandoned by its garrison.

But the United army, having snatched victory from defeat, as suddenly let the prize fall.

For seven hours they had charged and counter-charged in the heat of that June day. Many were wounded, but had fought on. Now they could fight no more. The victorious army suddenly dissolved into small parties of haggard men searching for food or spirits, or flinging themselves down to sleep where they lay.

Across the river, Johnson noticed the sudden lull. Finally the troops rallied. Back they poured across the bridge.

Little by little, the rebels were driven back to the Three Bullet Gate. An old man, or so it is said, cheerfully rushed ahead of the pikemen. Taking off his hat and wig, he thrust them up the cannon's barrel, calling: 'Blood-and-'ounds, my boys, come and take her now - she's stopt, she's stopt!' Next moment the gun blew him to atoms.

Courage and enthusiasm could not now win the day. At last the pikemen's charges became less vigorous as they were driven back once more through the gate. By six o'clock, all but a few had retreated to their camp, utterly exhausted.

In the town, however, the soldiers' work had only just begun.

'Formidable to everyone but the enemy' – Abercromby's bitter comment seemed entirely justified. The same men who had deserted Johnson at the moment of danger now returned to claim the wages of victory, paid in an orgy of looting and killing. Many of those the soldiers shot were wounded rebels; others were loyalists carelessly mistaken for rebels.

In the exceptional heat the rebel dead lay where they had fallen. Most of them, it was noticed, wore Catholic scapulars around their necks – small leather wallets with a suitable religious text inside.

Johnson himself had lost ninety-one men killed. No one knows how many rebels died; one of the lower contemporary estimates gave a total of 2,600.

Harvey, his days as Commander-in-Chief now over, returned despondently to Wexford to try

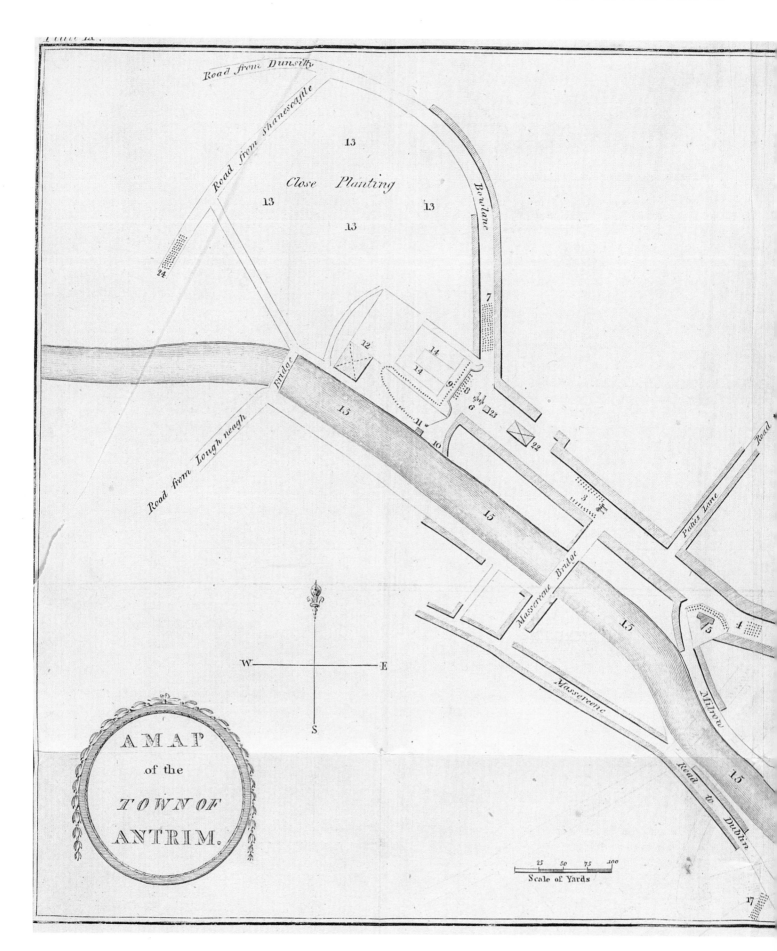

A MAP
of the
TOWN OF
ANTRIM.

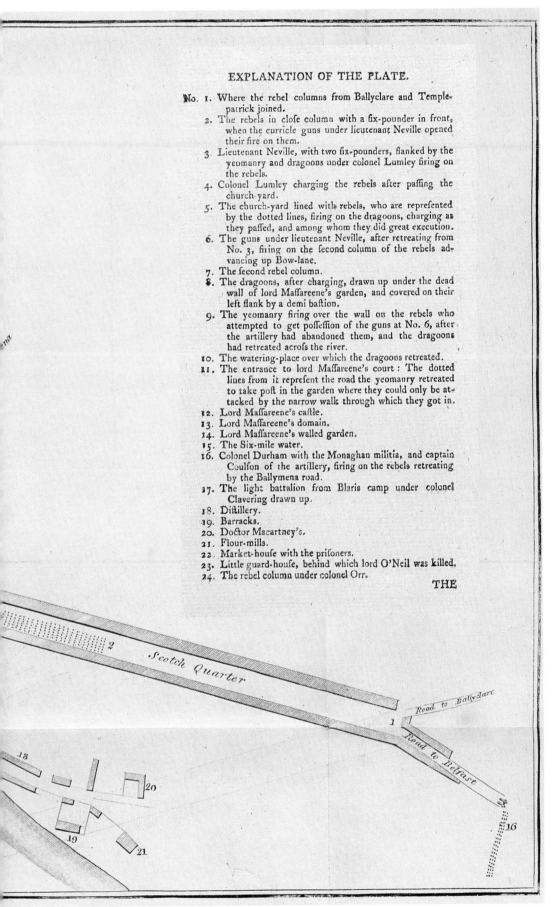

EXPLANATION OF THE PLATE.

No. 1. Where the rebel columns from Ballyclare and Temple-patrick joined.

2. The rebels in clofe column with a fix-pounder in front, when the curricle guns under lieutenant Neville opened their fire on them.

3. Lieutenant Neville, with two fix-pounders, flanked by the yeomanry and dragoons under colonel Lumley firing on the rebels.

4. Colonel Lumley charging the rebels after paffing the church-yard.

5. The church-yard lined with rebels, who are reprefented by the dotted lines, firing on the dragoons, charging as they paffed, and among whom they did great execution.

6. The guns under lieutenant Neville, after retreating from No. 3, firing on the fecond column of the rebels advancing up Bow-lane.

7. The fecond rebel column.

8. The dragoons, after charging, drawn up under the dead wall of lord Maffareene's garden, and covered on their left flank by a demi baftion.

9. The yeomanry firing over the wall on the rebels who attempted to get poffeffion of the guns at No. 6, after the artillery had abandoned them, and the dragoons had retreated acrofs the river.

10. The watering-place over which the dragoons retreated.

11. The entrance to lord Maffareene's court : The dotted lines from it reprefent the road the yeomanry retreated to take poft in the garden where they could only be attacked by the narrow walk through which they got in.

12. Lord Maffareene's caftle.

13. Lord Maffareene's domain.

14. Lord Maffareene's walled garden.

15. The Six-mile water.

16. Colonel Durham with the Monaghan militia, and captain Coulfon of the artillery, firing on the rebels retreating by the Ballymena road.

17. The light battalion from Blaris camp under colonel Clavering drawn up.

18. Diftillery.

19. Barracks.

20. Doctor Macartney's.

21. Flour-mills.

22. Market-houfe with the prifoners.

23. Little guard-houfe, behind which lord O'Neil was killed.

24. The rebel column under colonel Orr.

THE

2

Scotch Quarter

Road to Ballyclare

1

Road to Belfast

18

20

19

21

16

LEFT: *Plan of the town of Antrim during the battle on 7 June. From Musgrave's* **Rebellion** *(1801).*

what he could do for the imprisoned loyalists. Command in the field passed to Father Philip Roche, a huge, boisterous curate from mid-Wexford. He had little military understanding, but his size and strength, together with his authority as a priest, gave him a firm hold over the more wayward rebels.

It was, however, upon Perry and Fitzgerald's northern army – the Gorey division – that hopes of a United victory now chiefly depended. Their ambush of Walpole on 4 June, followed by Loftus's precipitate retreat, had presented them with a dazzling opportunity. Loftus had abandoned not only Gorey, but also Arklow, the key to the march northwards.

On 7 June, the Gorey division marched – but to Carnew, so that it was the 9th before they set off again. After one final delay, they at last came in sight of Arklow. Putting their hats on their pikes, they gave a wild cheer. Then they rushed on 'like madmen', waving the green flag.

Dublin and the North, 9–13 June

Strategically, the Castle felt their hands were completely tied until reinforcements came from England. Camden wrote another of his long, bitter complaints to London: unless they poured an 'immense' force into Ireland immediately, the country was lost.

His bitterness was understandable. He had asked for 10,000 men, the number Abercromby had regarded as the minimum necessary for the country's defence. Portland had promised 4,000. Now, in the third week of the rebellion, none would reach Ireland for at least another week.

In fact, Pitt and Portland *were* now finally convinced of the need to send 10,000 men. Before this decision could take effect, however, the situation in Ireland deteriorated further.

Two days after Antrim had risen, Down followed suit. By 11 June the whole north-eastern side of Ulster blazed with revolution.

McCracken had struck a confident note to his troops as they assembled on Donegore Hill, above Antrim, in the early hours of 7 June. But contingents had been left without leaders and isolated. Others were without proper arms or provisions.

Still, he did not need to rely on winning pitched battles. Simultaneous risings in Antrim and Down would spark off the risings in the rest of Ulster. Each village and town could be occupied by its local United corps, and as each garrison fell, the movement would snowball.

To attack Antrim successfully they must cut it off from the other garrisons – and thus from Government reinforcements – by securing the surrounding towns and villages. Meanwhile, the strategic centre of County Down, Ballynahinch, was to be attacked at the same time, while the other towns would be occupied by the respective contingents of each army.

What McCracken did not yet know was that the adjutant-general and colonels of County Down had been arrested a few hours before, and that General Nugent, forewarned by Magin, was sending reinforcements post-haste to Antrim. It was already clear, however, that plans had miscarried. Many contingents were missing: particularly the Catholic corps known as the Defenders, which had been only partly assimilated into the United movement.

Still, the army at Donegore Hill mustered at least 3,000, with more arriving every hour. There were further encouraging signs. Randalstown and Larne had both been captured almost without a shot, and the attacking forces were marching to join McCracken. By evening, virtually all the rest of the county, except around Carrickfergus and Belfast, had been taken.

About two o'clock, McCracken and some 6,000 United men marched into Antrim. The garrison – some 160 light dragoons, yeomen infantry and civilian volunteers – occupied two strongpoints: the market house, and Lord Massereene's castle beyond. McCracken sent one party to converge on the undefended church from the north; his column would advance towards it down the main street. The market house was to be attacked by the party from Randalstown.

He could not have known that Nugent now knew his plans, mainly from Magin's intelligence. McCracken relied completely on his allies in Down to fulfil their part of the plan. In fact, in the confusion caused by their general's arrest, there had been no rising there.

Worst of all, Crumlin, astride the road from the army camp at Blaris, was one of the few towns still in Government hands. As McCracken's forces stormed into Antrim, the vanguard of a strong reinforcement from Blaris galloped in from the opposite direction. At first the rebels won the advantage. But soon, with their only gun disabled, the attackers were pinned down by fire from the castle garden.

The Randalstown party, meanwhile, were met by some retreating cavalry. Somehow, the sight unnerved them: the retreat was mistaken for a

PRECEDING AND LEFT: *The Battle of Ballynahinch on 13 June by Thomas Robinson, the most detailed and authentic picture of a battle painted in 1798. Robinson, who lived nearby, shows the closing stages of the battle in Lord Moira's demesne at Montalto. The United army of Down has been broken by the cannonade of the King's troops; the dragoons turn rout into massacre; in the foreground Captain Evatt of the Monaghan militia lies mortally wounded; on the left the local yeomanry prepare to hang one of the rebel colonels, Hugh McCulloch, a grocer from Bangor; on the right (detail page 70) the victorious commander, General Nugent, waves to some dragoons riding in with the rebels' Liberty standards.*

ABOVE: 'The rebels executing
their prisoners on the bridge at
Wexford'. On 20 June, ninety-
seven loyalists were piked
and their bodies thrown in
the river. A Cruikshank
illustration (1845).

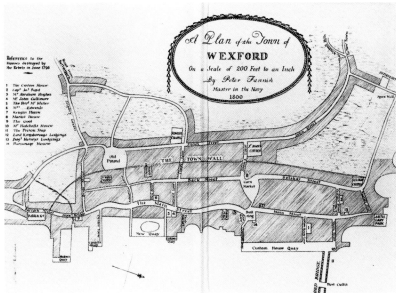

pursuit. In a moment the rebels had scattered. Soon the panic spread to McCracken's force.

Half an hour later, when the main body of reinforcements arrived, the battle was already over. Except for a small party still holding out in the churchyard (immortalized as the 'Spartan Band'), McCracken's whole army had fled.

The victors celebrated in the usual brutal fashion, killing innocent loyalists as well as rebels, wounded or unwounded. Some 300 rebels died, to the Government's 60 killed and wounded.

Despite this overwhelming victory, Nugent was left with a daunting task. Somehow he must crush the Antrim rising before it spread to adjacent Down, already stirring, and thence to Derry and Tyrone. Nor could he denude Belfast of troops without risking a rising there.

The solution was a brilliant piece of bluff. The commander of the reinforcements at Antrim had already received overtures from the rebels. He was now authorized to grant an amnesty. If all loyalist prisoners and all arms were surrendered, he would 'molest no one in the county'. But if these terms were not instantly accepted, 'he would set fire and totally destroy … every town, village and farmhouse … and put every one to the sword without any form of tryal whatever'. The rebels accepted the terms, and the rebellion in Antrim fizzled out as suddenly as it had begun.

Such terms were expedient as well as humane. For on 9 June, as the Antrim rising collapsed, the Down rising began.

On Magin's information, the Down general, Dickson, and all the colonels had been arrested two nights before. But while the army of Ulster

ABOVE: Plan of Wexford published in Musgrave's Rebellion (1801). The massacre of the prisoners took place on the bridge at lower right.

might be mortally wounded, it was still a formidable enemy. Nugent had little option but to adopt a strategy of extreme caution.

Its high command beheaded, Down had risen late, to Antrim's disadvantage. But it had risen. Newtownards had been taken on the night of the 8th, and on the following day many more towns were secured. Leaving garrisons, the United army of Down concentrated at Saintfield.

Their Commander-in-Chief was a young Lisburn draper, Henry Monroe. He had held no position in the United army hitherto, and now found himself trying to organize, almost single-handed, his insubordinate army of 7,000 men.

On Monday, 11 June one division was sent forward to Ballynahinch, where they pitched their camp at Montalto, Lord Moira's elegant estate. But behind the scenes the leaders were, as usual, divided over strategy. The north-east of the county was theirs. They had set up four camps – at Ballynahinch, Saintfield, Newtownards and Kilgobbin – and makeshift garrisons elsewhere; the rest of their army had now gathered at Montalto. They had been succssful in preventing outrages to loyalists and property.

Monroe was eager to show that they were strong and well disciplined enough to face regular troops, although others disagreed. Furthermore, the main body of Catholic Defenders had again shrunk back from joining. Those that had come resented Monroe's command.

Now, with these troubles still unresolved, the rebels saw what they most dreaded – a line of smoke to the north-west as Government troops marched towards them. In Down, Nugent had also issued a proclamation: the rebels must free their prisoners and abandon rebellion or the army would wreak 'indiscriminate vengeance' on them.

By Tuesday morning, with no response to his offer of amnesty, Nugent sent troops to cut off the rebels' line of retreat, while the Downpatrick commander, Colonel Stewart, was ordered to march his Scotch Fencibles to meet Nugent and the main army at Ballynahinch.

They closed the town on 10 June. The rebel front line was on Windmill Hill, although they were soon dislodged by a charge of the Scotch Fencibles. A protracted cannonade followed, which ended at about ten o'clock. As the night wore on large numbers of rebels deserted with their arms.

At first light Monroe sent some of his best pikemen into Ballynahinch, for in the narrow streets of the town they could exploit their num-bers – and the long pikes. They soon began to drive the soldiers back, killing or wounding about thirty of them, including their commander.

It was not enough. On the flank, Stewart and the Scotch Fencibles, with two guns, attacked the camp at Montalto. After driving in the rebel out-posts they approached the main body and, staying out of musket range, pounded away at their ranks with grapeshot. Time and again the rebels charged, only to be 'blown from the mouth of the cannon like chaff'.

At about seven in the morning, after some two hours of heavy fighting, they began to throw down their arms and run. Nugent's cavalry relentlessly turned defeat into rout, and rout into slaughter.

There was an official tally of captured arms, but no one could say how many rebels had been killed. It was assumed about 400. The bodies lay in the deserted streets of Ballynahinch, food for the local pigs.

By then Nugent's army had returned to Belfast, leaving Ballynahinch a smoking ruin – the funeral pyre of the short-lived Republic of Ulster.

London, 28 May – 22 June

In London, the crisis had forced Pitt to take a momentous decision.

The rebellion had proved Ireland's Government bankrupt in every sense. The kingdom could neither pay for, nor defend, itself. Since it could not, then England must take over the burden.

The first task was to remove Camden, who had shown he was not fit for his office, let alone the great political challenge ahead. Lake too was clearly inadequate. Why not combine Viceroy and Commander-in-Chief in one post? Pitt wasted no time. General the Marquess of Cornwallis had already been sounded.

Meanwhile, Pitt's arch-rival, Fox, was considering an Irish problem of a different kind.

On 7 June the Duke of Richmond heard from his sister, Lady Louisa Conolly, that their nephew – and Fox's cousin – Lord Edward Fitzgerald, had died of his wounds on the 4th. The news was the more distressing because he had been thought to be recovering.

Lord Edward's brother accused the Irish Government, and Camden in particular, of having murdered him by their ill treatment. But in fact the Government had done their utmost to be fair. He had been given the best room in Newgate, where he was attended by three

ABOVE: General John Moore, later to win fame in the Peninsular War, recaptured Wexford on 21 June. One of the more humane English generals in Ireland, he found his own Irish militia 'quite disgraceful'.

doctors. At first he seemed to be better, but the doctors were unable to extract the ball from his chest, and in the exceptionally hot weather the wounds turned septic.

If the Government had been heartless, it was only in forbidding his relations to visit him. But when it became obvious he was in great danger, Lord Clare himself had defied the ban and taken Lady Louisa and Lord Edward's brother, Lord Henry, to the prison in his own carriage. A few hours after they left, Lord Edward died.

In London, meanwhile, the Foxite Whigs were preparing to launch a new attack on Pitt's Irish policy: the rebellion, they maintained, was the result of 'tyranny', and the Administration must be censured accordingly.

Faced with Pitt's Coalition government, and an unreformed Parliament, the Foxite Whigs had theoretically given up Opposition in the middle of 1797, and ceased to attend Westminster. But now the rebellion, which confirmed their gloomiest forecasts, seemed to throw a new harsh light on the evil system which they had opposed for so long. For the moment their political appetite was restored. Even Fox, the most passionate advocate of the secession, was at last prepared to return to Westminster. The main debate on Ireland in the House of Commons was scheduled for 22 June.

The King remained his old self, moody and difficult. His resentment was particularly directed at the 'outrageous' disloyalty of his Irish subjects. Twice he had despondently agreed to the sending of British reinforcements to Ireland, despite the fact that it left England in a 'very naked state'. Nothing but 'the greatest necessity' could justify it. And he was now aware of how badly Ireland was governed. The present Viceroy was 'too agitated' and 'totally under the controul of the Irish Privy Councillors' – it was their rashness that had led to disaster.

Now he learned from Pitt that drastic changes were to be made. Cornwallis was to go to Ireland. His orders were to win the war; and to impose the settlement that both the King and his ministers had long regarded as the solution to the Irish problem – union with England.

In his reply, the King made a statement that was to be most ominous for the future: 'No indulgence can be granted to Catholics further than has been I am afraid inadvisedly done in former sessions.' Pitt's own view, however, was that the union of the two parliaments would remove the last rational obstacle to full emancipation. And whatever his misgivings about the King's attitude to Catholics, he had no doubts about the inability of the Irish Government to rule Ireland. On military grounds alone, the arguments were overwhelming.

Moreover, he and his inner cabinet agreed with the King that the Irish Privy Council or cabinet lay at the root of the problem. Everything that had occurred had only confirmed the urgent need for union – including the report of Bonaparte's plans to invade Ireland.

That question remained unresolved. Could Bonaparte really be heading for Ireland? And would Rear Admiral Sir Horatio Nelson, who in April had been sent with a fleet into the Mediterranean, succeed in stopping him?

It was now 22 June. After an audience with the King, Cornwallis embarked for Dublin. Pitt was left to repel the Foxites' parliamentary attack on his Irish policy. The motion was debated in secret, as it affected national security. But the war in Ireland had rallied the country behind Pitt, and he won one of his largest majorities.

Cornwallis would beat the rebels, of that Pitt had little doubt. But would the loyalists be as easily vanquished? For the moment, the plan for the Union was not to be divulged in Ireland.

Dublin and Wexford, 16–22 June

The Castle, however, could now see little military point in changing Viceroy, for the war in Wexford had quite unexpectedly changed for the better.

The turning point was reached when the Gorey division, some 19,000 strong, attacked Arklow. After two and a half hours of cannonade the attackers broke and fled, leaving two or three hundred bodies on the field.

So ended the third week of the rebellion, with no further reports of rebel attacks. The initiative returned to the Government.

General Lake's plan for the counter-attack in Wexford was simplicity itself. Five columns – over 10,000 men – under his personal command would converge on Enniscorthy, retake the town, and press on to Wexford. He made no mention, however, of rescuing the loyalist prisoners.

By 15 June everything was ready for the counter-attack – bar the still-missing reinforcements from Britain. These were essential, since they would reinforce the Dublin garrison, thereby allowing Lake to take his detachment of the Irish army south. And then, on the evening of the 16th, at long last the reinforcements arrived.

In Wexford, Keogh and the committee of public safety still held a precarious ascendancy over the mob. But every day brought new tales of Government atrocities, further inflaming the more vengeful rebels.

On the 14th the prisoners and the rebel leadership agreed to try to open hostage negotiations with the Government. The attempt failed miserably, however, when opponents of the plan turned the people's minds against it. The prisoners reached a new pitch of alarm. No one could now doubt the people's wish to murder them.

And now the army's progress, marked by a line of smoke, could be seen from the Three Rocks. Refugees poured into Wexford, bringing fresh tales of atrocities.

On the evening of the 19th Roche's New Ross division appeared, tattered and exhausted, at the Three Rocks. A few hours later all the pikemen and musketeers in Wexford itself were ordered to join Roche there. The town was to be left to the prisoners, their guards, various non-combatants, and the refugees. And then, on the following morning, Thomas Dixon – a sea captain who was notorious for his anti-loyalist views and actions – led a vast mob up to the gates of the gaol.

Only one member of Keogh's committee cared to intervene, in desperation trying to arrange a makeshift trial for the prisoners. But

Hessian Dragoons '98 Insurrection

*Dragoons in the Irish
bellion of 1798.*

ABOVE: *William Sadler's dramatic reconstruction of
a calvary charge in 1798, painted in the 1880s.
The Hessians were German mercenaries, notorious for
atrocities against unarmed men and women. Against the
pike, courageously used, they could make less headway.*

View of VINEGAR HILL on the North east side.

1. Light Infantry with Howitzer.   4 & 5 Gen. Dundas's Brigade.   8 Rebels Fort of Vinegar Hill.
2. Gen. Lake where his Horse was Killed.   6 Gen. Loftus's Brigade.   9 Rebel Lines & forest of Pikes.
3. Gen. Wilford's Brigade.   7 Gen. Sr. Js. Duff's Brigade.   10 Enniscorthy side of the Slaney.

1. Pike for cutting and stabbing.
2. Do. for stabbing only.
3. Do. for grappling and stabbing.

A Scapular.

Dixon plied the people with whiskey, then took two of the loyalists and persuaded them, in return for their lives, to make 'a full confession' of the Orange plot at Wexford. News of this sent the people into a frenzy.

The prisoners were hustled down the street to the Custom House Quay beside the bridge, where a 'tribunal' was established by Dixon. Each prisoner was charged, and unless he could prove that he had helped the people, received sentence of death. The chief prosecutor was Dixon. The mob was judge.

For two hours the dreadful ritual continued. Each victim was led out on to the bridge and told to kneel down. Ninety-seven prisoners lay dead on the planks or in the water below, ripped open by the pikes of the executioners.

And then, about five o'clock, as the last three men of a batch were made to kneel down, one of the rebel leaders galloped up and ordered them to beat to arms. The Vinegar Hill camp was beset – every man needed to defend it. The pikemen marched away immediately and the mob dispersed. Soon there was no-one on the bridge but the three prisoners, still kneeling. Then their gaolers returned to escort them back to prison.

That night, thoroughly alarmed, Keogh's committee and the prisoners agreed on a common front in their desperate situation.

The plan was that Lord Kingsborough would take possession of Wexford in the name of the King, on condition of protection for the town and its inhabitants, except those guilty of murder. Three pairs of emissaries, one for each of the armies approaching Wexford, would take a letter from Kingsborough to the Government.

Early next morning the emissaries rode away on their perilous mission, leaving the loyalists between hope and despair. The people appeared to accept the surrender; yet there was still Dixon, and others like him, to contend with.

It had taken the Government armies four days to reach and encircle Vinegar Hill, and even now, on the morning of the fifth day, General Needham had not come up. Lake did not bother to wait for him.

About seven the cannon opened up a brisk bombardment on the 20,000 wretched rebels herded together on the summit. For an hour, the pikemen manfully withstood the fire. The fighting was fiercest in Enniscorthy itself. Slowly the rebel pikemen retreated up the cobbled streets, inflicting heavy casualties on the soldiers as they went. But soon both rebel forces broke and fled through the gap that Needham had still failed to close – along the road to Wexford.

When the pursuit was called off, after perhaps 500 fugitives had been cut down, Lake's army celebrated in the usual style. In Enniscorthy, the troops burnt a makeshift hospital, wounded rebels and all.

Meanwhile Lake remained sublimely indifferent to the fate of the Wexford loyalists. When two of the emissaries appeared, he first kept them waiting twelve hours, then replied that he could not 'attend to any terms of surrender by rebels :...'.

Fortunately, not all generals acted as Lake did. On the morning of 20 June, General Moore had marched from New Ross, following the southern division of Roche's army as it retreated towards Wexford.

At a place called Foulk's Mill he fought a brisk action with a rebel force much larger than his own, an engagement which would certainly have ended in disaster if Moore had not several times personally taken command when his men wavered. Eventually the rebels were driven off with heavy casualties.

Lake had instructed Moore to halt well short of Wexford. Next morning the second pair of emissaries rode up, and Moore immediately grasped what Lake had ignored: the loyalists' predicament. He decided, against orders, to march to the relief of the town, even though his force was still heavily outnumbered.

As they approached Wexford, Moore halted the main force and sent 200 British regulars into the town. Ahead of them galloped a dozen Wexford yeomen, hardly daring to hope they would find any of their friends and relations alive.

The rebels Moore had beaten poured into the town vowing vengeance on all Protestants. The loyalists prepared themselves for a massacre.

There then came a general cry, 'The Army are come!' At that the rebels ran, 5,000 men perhaps, headed, people said later, by Captain Dixon on a white horse.

Next morning, Lake marched in triumph into the town. What he was incapable of recognizing, however, was that his own blockheaded pursuit of military victory, and his insistence on 'severe examples', had dispersed, not extinguished, the Wexford rising.

Despairing of terms, the rebels streamed north from the town, past the burnt-out farms and dead refugees, one army making for Carlow, the other for the Wicklow Mountains, but both still trapped in the vicious circle of atrocity and reprisal.

FAR LEFT: General Lake's botched victory over the rebels at Vinegar Hill, outside Enniscorthy, on 21 June. It was followed by a massacre of wounded rebels in a makeshift hospital. The print, with details of pikes and a scapular worn by rebels, was published in Musgrave's Rebellion (1801).

Dublin Militia   *Royal Dublin Militia Band*

Queen's Own Royal Dublin Militia going into Action at Vinegar Hill the Light company

LEFT: A reconstruction by William Sadler of the Battle of Vinegar Hill painted in about 1880. Well-directed artillery gave the British regulars and Irish militia a crushing advantage against pikemen.

OLIVE

PART
FOUR

**Dublin and Leinster,
22 June–21 July**

ALTHOUGH he had surrendered Yorktown during the war in America, Cornwallis had won a reputation as a strategist and negotiator, and had since held a series of important imperial, military and cabinet posts. Now fifty-nine, he was in indifferent health; nor was he enthusiastic about his new appointment. To Pitt, however, he seemed uniquely qualified, both as soldier and statesman, to bring peace to Ireland.

In the Castle and among the cabinet, there was grumbling about Camden's removal, and about the new Viceroy's well-known sympathy for Catholics. Cornwallis, however, simply ignored such people. The old cabinet of Foster, Beresford and the rest were simply not consulted. The day-to-day civil administration was left to Cooke and the other secretaries, and control of the wild Irish Parliament to Castlereagh.

After a week in Ireland Cornwallis already knew the worst. The rebels' violence and religious intolerance, coupled with the 'ferocity of our troops who delight in murder', blocked all plans for conciliation.

In Wexford, Lake had let loose the army. In seven days, his brutal methods of 'pacification' had spread the war across the adjoining counties. Worse, his policy – effectively, one of looting, burning and murder by the military – had created new adversaries out of the shattered rebel armies.

BRANCH

LEFT: Lord Cornwallis, who succeeded Lord Camden as Viceroy in mid June, was determined to impose peace on Ireland. But he found the 'ferocity of our troops who delight in murder most powerfully counteracts all plans for conciliation'.

His attitude to rebels trying to surrender made the situation worse. Many people, believing that he had endorsed Kingsborough's terms, had left the two Wexford armies and were awaiting official protection. Their effective Commander-in-Chief, Father Roche, deciding he would try to negotiate, rode back to Wexford on 22 June.

Legally, the rebel leaders were guilty of treason. Yet there was a strong case for clemency: few had wanted the rising, far less its brutality. For Lake, however, only 'severe examples' would serve. Accordingly Father Roche was beaten, tried by summary court martial, and hanged three days later on Wexford bridge.

Nor did the General take any account of degrees of responsibility among the leaders, Protestant or Catholic. Sentenced to death, Keogh made an eloquent speech protesting he had never been a United man, which moved Moore to try to persuade Lake to stay the execution – but without success. Keogh was hanged.

Other gentlemen caught up in the rebellion – Harvey and Colclough – had believed that their claims to have acted under duress would be accepted. Both protested their innocence, although they admitted their membership of the United movement. They too were hanged.

Lake now announced that he would give the 'deluded' masses a final chance of surrender if they brought in their arms within three days, and either gave their leaders up or revealed their whereabouts. Failure to accept these terms would, he promised, bring 'just vengeance'.

In the three weeks of the Irish Republic at Wexford, the rebels had heard not one word from the Dublin Executive.

Now they learned at last the shattering truth. The rebellion had failed. Many, despairing of being able to surrender, clung instead to the hope of linking up with United armies elsewhere.

The two Wexford armies now separated – the northern contingent under Perry and Fitzgerald heading for the mountains, the western army, led by Father John Murphy, for the central plain. The latter, in particular, had hopes of raising the country as they went. Yet the people distrusted them, and none joined. At length, exhausted, short of food and, above all, ammunition, the survivors doubled back into Wicklow, having marched through five counties in the space of a week – all for nothing. They found the northern army in little better state.

The hard core of the United army, including Perry and Fitzgerald, now decided to try to link up with the United forces in Kildare. They would make a last forlorn attempt to raise the 100,000 United men in the counties around Dublin.

Cornwallis, first and foremost, was determined to stamp out arbitrary floggings and hangings by yeomen and magistrates. No punishment whatever must be inflicted without confirmation by a general after a properly constituted court martial.

In the first week of July Cornwallis instructed his generals to offer amnesty to the rank and file on significantly more humane terms than Lake's. Nor, when that failed, did he flinch from a general amnesty – that is, for leaders as well as rank and file. Leaders would be offered their lives, though they would be liable to exile – the only exception to be the handful guilty of 'cool and deliberate murder'. The problem, however, lay in carrying this measure with Parliament and Privy Council.

The hard core of the Privy Council were the cabinet – the real rulers of Ireland for a decade. Seeing Cornwallis now governed without them, their clamour against the new pardon grew. Worse, they sought to thwart the Viceroy in Parliament.

For Cornwallis, rescue came from an unexpected quarter: the Chancellor. As senior law officer his help was vital. And what gave Clare his peculiar political weight in this case was that he had been consistently the most articulate spokesman against concessions for Catholics. Nor had these prejudices softened. But he believed that Ireland's place was in union with Britain. Moreover, he had no doubt that the Constitution's real enemy was godless Jacobinism, not Catholicism. Now, ignoring his cabinet colleagues, he let it be known he heartily approved of the amnesty.

The new partnership flourished. Together Cornwallis and Clare planned to settle the rebels with the amnesty, and the loyalists with a series of treason trials. But first they must end the guerrilla war in Wicklow and Kildare. For now there was the serious threat that the fugitives from Wexford might join up with their fellows in Kildare.

It was an uncomfortable fact that after holding out for a month, the Kildare rebel army had achieved only one of their aims: to stay alive. From their stronghold at Timahoe they had survived by raiding. They had received no reinforcements from Meath or Wicklow, no instructions from Dublin, no help from France. Now their situation was desperate.

In early July their leader, William Aylmer, tried to arrange terms of surrender. But on the 10th, before anything could be agreed, Wexford and Wicklow rebels suddenly appeared on the scene.

LEFT: *The unfortunate Henry Sheares. With his brother John, he was arrested before the rising, convicted of high treason in July, and hanged in Dublin.*

Nightly Visitors, at St Ann's Hill; — {"In glided Edwards pale-eyed Ghost, And stood at Carlo's feet."

The armies split up again almost immediately, the Wexford and Wicklow men to march northwards, the Kildare rebels to remain in order to try to negotiate a surrender. Once again the hopes of forming a real provincial army out of different county forces had proved vain.

The surviving Wexford rebels marched on, still refusing to believe that the Midlands – the counties best organized by the Executive – would not rally to them. On they went through Meath and into Louth, and still no one joined them. And all the way the yeomanry and regulars were snapping at their heels, till the army of 2,000 had been reduced to a few hundred starving, desperate men, who ten days later struggled back towards Kildare.

On 20 July, the last of the United armies in the field officially surrendered, the rank and file receiving protection, the leaders, including Aylmer and Fitzgerald, being sent to Dublin, the first captured leaders since the outbreak of the rebellion to escape execution. By ill luck Perry and Father Kearns returned too late under the terms of the surrender. Taken by yeomanry, they were hanged.

In the meantime, a great change had come over Ireland. In the teeth of the hangin'-shootin'-and-burnin' gentlemen, Cornwallis had pushed his amnesty through Parliament.

The four provinces, 21 July– 24 August

Even the loyalists could see some sense in the amnesty. Quite simply, the prisons were full – and they could not hang and shoot half the nation.

The eighty-two state prisoners arrested in March were lodged in relative comfort in the main Dublin prisons. Aylmer and thirteen other Kildare prisoners had been sent to the Royal Exchange – a coffee house requisitioned as a yeomanry barracks. The mass of ordinary prisoners were not so lucky – some thrown in the Provost, a military prison, the bulk shipped off to the equally crowded and disease-ridden tenders in Dublin Bay.

There was, however, one consolation for the Dublin prisoners: they had some chance of a fair hearing. The majority of rebels tried since the outbreak had been found not guilty, and fewer than a dozen in the entire region were to be executed. In general, the Dublin garrison could claim to be doing their best.

Not so the garrisons responsible for justice in other areas. This was quite simply because the Irish army had been free to administer justice as they liked – that army whose 'favourite pastime', according to Cornwallis, was murder.

Like the rest of this year's horrors, the responsibility was Camden's, if not Pitt's. But the policy was Lake's: that of 'giving the Irish army its head' in order to crush the rising. Unhindered, they had used hanging and flogging as the means.

Such inadequate records as Cornwallis had gave a total of 106 United Irishmen sentenced to death that year, and 268 to transportation. (The real total of executions is probably twice that number, to which must be added those executed without even the pretence of a trial.) Strangely, the Presbyterian North suffered the most executions – thirty-four in all, including McCracken and Monroe.

The one redeeming feature was that in many areas there were officers and gentlemen, like Moore, who accepted the need for clemency. Yet for every loyalist in the threatened areas who disapproved of the policy, there were a hundred who felt it to be grossly lenient.

Most of the eighty-two state prisoners were in no danger from ordinary process of law, however. Even Reynolds's evidence was sufficient to commit only three – Bond, his secretary, McCann, and the Wicklow delegate, William Byrne. With the possible exception of Neilson, only two others could be prosecuted, Henry and John Sheares. Cornwallis therefore had two choices – to try these five and abandon hope of prosecuting all the rest of those chiefly responsible for the rebellion, or to use other methods. He was not, however, the man to allow 'severity beyond the law'. In mid-July he authorized the Castle to proceed as best they could with the treason trials.

The Sheares brothers were the first to be tried. Given the evidence of Armstrong, who stood up well to the battering of the defence, and with the Crown's case further strengthened by John Sheares's captured proclamation, it took the jury just seventeen minutes to find both guilty. They were executed at Newgate the next day.

The second batch of trials proved equally heartening. This time the key prosecution witness was Reynolds. Though the defence denounced him with astonishing ferocity, once again the Crown witness cut a good figure in the jury's eyes; loyalists saw nothing wrong in his actions. McCann, Byrne and Bond were found guilty.

The state prisoners' bluff had been called. In their gaols urgent meetings were held. After McCann's execution on 24 July, a round robin was signed putting a remarkable offer to the Government. Without implicating individuals they would agree to give full details of the United

FAR LEFT: Charles James Fox, the British leader of the opposition, supposed to have corrupted his cousin, Lord Edward Fitzgerald, whose ghost haunts him in his villa near London, together with the headless bodies of the Sheares brothers and other conspirators. A caricature by Gillray (1798).

ABOVE: *In mid-July the survivors of the Wexford and Wicklow armies tried to cut their way through to the Midlands. But 2,000 rebels were repulsed by twenty-seven yeomen in a fortified post at Clonard, County Meath. A scene from Cruikshank (1845).*

movement and of its links with allies overseas. In return they should all be allowed to emigrate. The letter was presented to the Castle on 26 July, the day appointed for the fourth execution – Byrne's.

For Cornwallis, as for Cooke and Castlereagh, the proposition was extraordinarily tempting. Other law officers, however, opposed even a stay of execution to examine the offer more carefully.

Unfortunately, Clare was away ill, and under the circumstances Cornwallis felt he had no choice but to let the law take its course. Byrne was hanged.

Next day Bond was to be executed. Frantically the prisoners made the terms more specific. Cornwallis and Cooke were still more strongly in favour of accepting. But how to carry their own supporters, let alone the public, who were baying for blood? Already there was an outcry in Dublin at the prospect of negotiation.

At this critical moment the Chancellor returned – to announce in Parliament that it would be 'inexcusable' to reject the offer. The outcry died down, and the pact was signed between the seventy-eight surviving prisoners and the Government.

A week later the 'Kilmainham Deputies' – Emmet, McNevin, O'Connor, Bond and Neilson – produced a forty-page memoir of their plans for revolution. There was little new to the Government in the document, but here were the authors of the conspiracy freely confessing to all the charges that they and their Whig champions in England and Ireland had long denied.

This memoir, and its counterpart in the replies the state prisoners made to the secret committee of the Lords and Commons, admitted that the real aim of the United Irish movement was to establish an independent democratic republic. All talk of constitutional redress of grievances had been 'mere pretence'. It was equally frank about their methods. Physical force was the only way of achieving independence. This had been agreed in 1796, the year in which a military alliance was made with Britain's enemy, France.

Cornwallis wrote to London that they had won a 'complete triumph'.

By mid-August, peace seemed within reach at length. With the news that the Wicklow resistance had petered out, Cornwallis was now politically on the crest of a wave.

Moore's return from Wicklow – which he had swiftly subdued with those revolutionary weapons, elementary humanity and military discipline – seemed to signify the end of the war. It had lasted almost exactly three months, and cost perhaps 30,000 lives.

One mystery remained unsolved, however. What had happened to Bonaparte's armada? It was clearly not bound for Ireland. Yet spy reports from France still maintained an invasion was imminent. The latest, dated 3 August, reported a substantial fleet in Brest with a considerable number of troops – all destined for Ireland.

Cornwallis could now cast his mind to the Union, though he confessed he could not see the 'the most distant encouragement'. Only a handful of Irishmen were in the secret, but even the most fervent among them, like Clare, saw no prospect of carrying it with the loyalists in their present state. For a consideration, the hangin'-shootin'-and-burnin' gentlemen might sell their own political birthright to Britain. But nothing would ever induce them to sell it to help the Catholics.

If there was one loyal province, it was Connaught. There had been reports of United activity, but there was certainly no regular United organization. The province was the poorest and most backward in Ireland; land hunger was endemic, with inevitable tensions between landlord and tenant. Yet so far there seemed to have been no serious attempt to exploit these grievances politically. Accordingly Connaught had been left in peace by the army and the magistrates.

Killala, on the northern coast of County Mayo, seemed even less likely to be dragged into revolution. But on 22 August there was something of a sensation in the little town. For in the bay were three frigates, flying British colours, although they were in fact French. That evening, a French general rode up to the 'castle', a half-ruined pile in which lived the local bishop, Dr Joseph Stock, and broke the news to the Bishop in person. They had come to liberate them from the 'English yoke'.

Reports that the French had arrived at last sent a shudder through the capital, but two days passed without any sign of risings. Cornwallis, however, was taking no chances. He had seen enough of the Irish army to agree with Abercromby's damning verdict. He had also good reason to think that the Killala force was only the first instalment of a sizeable French expedition. And there was a confidential report from Mayo that 5,000 peasantry had joined the invaders.

Before leaving to take command of the troops dispatched to crush the French, he wrote to Portland that more reinforcements might be needed. With Ireland in its present state, a single check could be 'fatal in its consequences'.

ABOVE: The French are on the sea, says the Shan Van Vocht. But was it all too late? William Sadler's reconstruction (1880) of Humbert's troop landing at Killala on 22 August.

French-occupied Mayo, and France, August 1798 and before

The 1,099 officers and men who had landed at Killala were indeed only the advance guard of a sizeable French armada. They had sailed from La Rochelle on 6 August, to coincide with the sailing of a force of some 3,000 men from Brest, commanded by a senior French general, Hardy, and including Wolfe Tone; there was to be a small expedition from Dunkirk; and a further 4,000 were to follow as soon as circumstances allowed.

Their own commander was General Joseph Humbert. Once a dealer in animal skins, he had risen rapidly in the Revolutionary army. He had served with Hoche, sailed with him on the abortive Bantry Bay expedition and been rescued from the wreck of the *Droits de l'homme*. Now, a veteran of thirty-one, he was to be given another chance to test the idea that the place to attack Britain was at her weakest point – Ireland.

The Directory's orders were for Humbert's expedition 'to convey to Ireland arms and ammunition' in order to 'help the United Irish … throw off the English yoke'. But Hardy and Humbert were not to intervene in the main insurrection directly. Having established a base, Humbert was to find Hardy and place himself under his orders. If Hardy had not yet landed, he was to await him. In any event he was to act with 'the greatest caution' until he had either joined Hardy or rallied enough Irishmen 'for important operations'.

At Brest, however, Hardy's fleet had still not put to sea. Delayed first by bureaucracy, then by adverse winds, and then by the British blockade, on 26 August Hardy was instructed to postpone the enterprise until the autumn gales broke that blockade. Worse, all idea of sending the succeeding expedition of 4,000 men was now abandoned.

For Tone, the delays were the culmination of a crushing series of disappointments. His misgivings about Bonaparte's sincerity had proved well founded, for on 26 May he had learned that the General had embarked with the Toulon fleet for 'distant seas'.

Three days before, unknown to anyone in France, the rebellion had broken out in Ireland.

One of the difficulties United Irish exiles in France faced was that they had split into hostile groups. Tone's friends now boycotted Napper Tandy and his supporters, both groups claiming to act with the authority of the United movement.

When news of the rising reached France early in June, the exiles at once appealed to the Directory for an immediate expedition to Ireland

PRECEDING PAGES: The revolutionary army in action. A detail from a contemporary picture of Napoleon's victory at the Battle of the Pyramids in 1798. However, he sent Humbert to Ireland with only 1,099 officers and men.

LEFT: 'Heroic conduct of the Highland Sentinel'. Cruikshank's picture (1845) of an act of heroism at the Battle of Castlebar. But most of Lake's army ran away.

THE ALLIED REPUBLICS OF FRANCE AND IRELAND

LIBERTY AND ERIN GO BRAY EQUALITY

To the Tune of Moll Brook

From Brest in de Bay of Biskey
me come for de very fine Whiskey
to make de Jacobin fruskey
While Erin may go bray
    While Erin may go bray
    While Erin may go bray
Me have got de mealy Pattato
From de Irish Democrato
To make de Jacobin fat o
    While Erin may go bray

I get by de Guillotine Axes
De Wheats & de Oats & de Flaxes
De Rents & de Tides & de Taxes
While Erin may go bray
    While Erin may go bray.
    While Erin may go bray.
I put into Requisition
De Girl of ev'ry condition
For Jacobin Coalition
    And Erin may go bray

De linen I get in de Scuffle
Will make de fine Shirt to my ruffle
While Pat may go starve in his Hovel
And Erin may go bray
    And Erin may go bray
    And Erin may go bray
De Beef is good for my Belly
De Calf make very fine Jelly
For me to kiss Nora & Nelly
    And Erin may go bray

Fitzgerald & Artur ó Conner
To Erin have done de great Honor
To put me astride upon her
For which she now does bray
    For which she now does bray
    For which she now does bray
She may figet & Caper & kick o
But by de good help of old Nick o
De Jacobin ever will stick o
    And Erin may go bray

Pub. Oct.r 17 1798 by S.W. Fores N°50 Piccadilly

of at least 1,000 men. The French responded with their far more ambitious scheme, Tone agreeing that there was little point in sending a small force.

Napper Tandy's faction disagreed. Tandy declared that he had himself only to land in Ireland for 30,000 men to rise. The Directory, impressed, next month assigned Tandy a fast corvette to test his claims .

But as the weeks passed, both Tone and Tandy could see that unless Humbert achieved a miracle, the Irish revolution would be over before either of their expeditions could arrive.

Meanwhile, Humbert had begun the advance into the interior, brushing aside the feeble forces opposing him. His problems lay with his new allies. The United Irish in France had led them to expect the country to rise in arms to shake off the oppressor's yoke. Yet of the respectable inhabitants, only two Protestants had come forward, both drunks. The Catholics who flocked to join them all seemed to be ignorant peasants, of little use in forming a provisional government.

The French did not stint the supply of arms and uniforms – few of the Irish cared that the latter were odds and ends scrounged from the magazine at La Rochelle. The guns all but defeated them, to the frustration of the French. The levies mishandled the muskets, sometimes breaking them, and profligately wasted powder and shot. They ceased to be issued with ball when a shot discharged by an awkward recruit narrowly missed Humbert.

Humbert's men did their best to respect the idiosyncrasies of their allies, as the Directory had ordered. They found the experience profoundly disheartening.

On 25 August, Humbert advanced to Ballina, leaving 200 men to secure his line of retreat. His veterans found the local yeomanry easy meat. Their nerve broken after a skirmish, these retreated to Foxford, abandoning Ballina without a shot.

Humbert was too flamboyant a character to wait while his enemies closed around him, and besides, there was little chance of his Irish levies reaching a state that would allow him to act independently of Hardy. But he also had orders to precipitate a rising, and how better than by some daring feat of arms? He had just learned that some 3,500 regulars were advancing towards him. There was only one chance: to strike at their position at Castlebar while they were still off balance.

He left Ballina on the afternoon of the 26th, with 700 French infantry and cavalry, about the same number of Irish levies, and a single cannon.

The Surrender of the French General Humbert To General Lake at Ballinamuck. September. 8.th 1798.

LEFT: General Lake accepts General Humbert's sword as a token of surrender at Ballinamuck. Less chivalrous was Lake's treatment of France's Irish allies captured after the battle.

As well as the road to Castlebar through Foxford, he learned that there was another, barely more than a track, leading through the wildest part of the district. It was quite undefended, while the bridge at Foxford was now blocked by a substantial garrison. Following the road for a few miles, he dodged back and took the mountain track.

They marched all night until, in the small hours, they at last saw Castlebar ahead of them – 'a tough nut to crack,' as one officer commented. The British had dug trenches astride the only possible approach to the town, and had brought up artillery.

After stationing a garrison at Foxford, the commander at Castlebar, Major-General John Hely-Hutchinson, was left with only about 1,700 troops, the great majority Irish militia, with a small force of Scotch Fencibles, some dragoons and yeomanry, and a detachment from a line regiment. His strongest card was his artillery – ten curricle guns and a howitzer. Having been warned by Cornwallis not to attempt any advance with so small a force, he had prepared a defensive position to the north-west of the town. At eleven o'clock that night Lake, sent on post-haste by Cornwallis, arrived and assumed overall command.

FAR LEFT: 'Erin Go Bray'. ('Ireland for ever'.) An English caricature drawn by Samson in 1798, showing the benefits that the alliance with France had brought Ireland.

Connaught and Leinster, 27 August – 30 September

That day, 27 August, Cornwallis and his staff had reached Athlone. The news he had half expected came in the night: a French triumph at Castlebar.

The military losses – as well as the troops' behaviour during their flight – were bad enough. The strategic repercussions were incalculable. There were already signs of a rising in Kildare and Meath, and a general insurrection might follow.

But while Humbert was reported to be digging in at Castlebar, Cornwallis's forces continued to accumulate at Tuam; by 2 September they totalled 7,800 men. To raise such an army, he had cut the garrisons of Ireland as much as he dared. If, as the Government now thought likely, Leinster rose again, everything would depend on the gentry. It was not a comforting thought.

The longer the French went undefeated, the greater the danger of such a rising. And there was a second, more chilling, danger. Humbert was said to be expecting the Brest expedition any day.

His army might seem large, but Cornwallis had no illusions about his men. He could not afford to take the smallest unnecessary risk. The troops he had were 'bad and undisciplined … the least check and the country was gone.'

For Humbert, the results of his victory had been dramatic. Among other benefits, the British had retired to Sligo and Boyle. Furthermore, the country people from miles around flocked to his standard; although the calibre of the gentlemen he had relied on to officer his levies was less heartening. The choice of their commander proved especially unfortunate – when he had first tried to join the yeomanry defending Castlebar, it seemed he had been rejected as a hopeless alcoholic.

Given such officers, the Irish corps took to plundering the houses and estates of prominent local loyalists, also vandalizing a Protestant church. To cap it all, some began to complain of ill treatment by the French: it was unfair to make them surrender their loot; they felt discriminated against in matters like rations and lodgings, they resented the menial tasks set them by French officers. Humbert finally lost patience: two Irish captains were taken out and shot – and order was restored.

In his official dispatches to the Directory that week, he emphasized the bright side. (Although to the Minister of Marine he admitted his disappointment at Irish levies.) But he needed 2,000 more French troops – artillery, infantry, cavalry – for he now saw that if he was to achieve anything, it could only be by French arms.

ABOVE: General Napper Tandy, Tone's bitter rival. He boasted that 30,000 would rise to join him when he set foot in Ireland.

FAR RIGHT: 'After several unsuccessful attempts behold at last Frenchmen among you.' Humbert's high-flown proclamation to the peasants of Mayo in August. Whatever they made of it, 5,000 joined his standard.

Early in the morning of the 27th came the bizarre news that a large group of men 'in blue uniforms' was marching down the rocky track. At eight, the French column appeared over the ridge, and Lake ordered the cannonade to begin, hoping that the enemy column would be broken by grapeshot before coming within musket range of his line. He would then unleash his cavalry.

Humbert recognized his desperate situation now that he had lost the element of surprise. His veterans, however, did not flinch. The Grenadiers charged forward. Still out of musket range, their own gun disabled and with mounting casualties, Humbert learned that most of his Irish levies had fled. And it was at this moment that the Irish levies on the other side – the militia – achieved what even their greatest detractors would have believed impossible. They turned and ran.

The French Grenadiers charged the guns and carried them at bayonet-point. A few of the rear-guard fought gallantly, the officers struggling to rally the main garrison. But nothing could check the wild, primitive terror that the French inspired. In their eagerness to escape, all cannon, all their munitions, even Lake's luggage, were left behind. The soldiers did not pause till they reached Tuam, thirty miles way, some pressing on to Athlone. So ended the 'Races of Castlebar', one of the most ignominious defeats in British military history.

ERTY, EQUALITY, FRATERNITY, UNIO

IRISHMEN,

YOU have not forgot Bantry bay. You know what efforts France has made to assist you.

Her affection for you, her desire of avenging your wrongs and assuring your independence can never be impaired.

After several unsuccessfull attempts, behold at last Frenchmen arrived amongst you.

They come to support your courage, to share your dangers, to join their arms and to mix their blood with yours in the sacred cause of liberty.

They are the forerunners of other Frenchmen, whom you shall soon enfold in your arms.

Brave IRISHMEN, our cause is common. Like you we abhor the avaricious and blood-thirsty policy of an oppressive governement. Like you we hold as indefeasible the right of all nations to liberty. Like you we are persuaded that the peace of the world shall ever be troubled as long as the British ministry is suffered to make with impunity a traffic of the industry, labour and blood of the people.

But exclusive of the same interests which unite us, we have powerfull motives to love and defend you.

Have we not been the pretext of the cruelty exercised against you by the Cabinet of St. James? The heart-felt interest you have shown for the grand events of our revolution, has it not been imputed to you as a crime? Are not tortures and death continually hanging over such of you as are barely suspected of being our friends?

Let us unite then and march to glory.

We Swear the most inviolable respect for your properties, your laws and all your religions opinions. Be free, be masters in your own country. We look for no other conquest than that of your Liberty, no other success than yours.

The_____aking your chains is arrived. Our triumphant troops are now flying_____ties of the earth to tear up the roots of the wealth and tyranny of_____. That frightfull colossus is mouldering away in every part. Can_____ny Irishman base_____ough to seperate himself in such a happy conjunct_____in the grand in_____of his country. If su_____re be, brave friends, let him be chased from the_____try he betrays and let his property become the reward of those generous men who know how to fight and die.

Irishmen, recollect the late defeats wich your ennemies have experienced from the French; recollect the plains of Honscoote, Toulon, Quiberon and Ostende; recollect America free from the moment she wished to be so. The contest between you and your oppressors can not be long.

Union, Liberty, the Irish Republic. Such is our shout. Let us march. Our hearts are devoted to you; our glory is in your happiness.

ABOVE: Admiral Warren's ships pounding the Brest fleet of General Hardy after intercepting it off Lough Swilly. The French – and their Irish allies – fought with desperate courage. The British captured most of Hardy's fleet, took 2,500 prisoners, including adjutant-general Smith, alias Wolfe Tone.

It was not entirely surprising that Humbert's triumph did not precipitate risings elsewhere. Beyond Connaught, most of Leinster had had its fill of rebellion, though some United leaders had tried to reorganize for a rising. In both Longford and Westmeath, however, the movement had remained hidden like an unexploded bomb. Humbert's success was enough to detonate it.

Fruen Hill lies on the borders of these two counties. At about eleven in the morning of 4 September several hundred country people, many armed with pikes, marched there and formed a camp, their numbers growing all the while.

Eight miles to the east, at Mullingar, the garrison was defenceless. The local magistrate had been told that a rising was imminent, but most of the troops had been sent to join Cornwallis, and the loyalists were without arms.

The same morning, ten miles the other side of Fruen Hill, men with pikes were seen marching on Edgeworthstown. The nearest garrison town could spare no help. The rebels continued to pour across from Westmeath into County Longford.

Meanwhile Humbert was marching away towards Sligo, hoping to evade the British and press on to link up with insurgents in Ulster. At the same time, unknown to him, another strategic development was taking place.

On 27 August the French corvette *Anacréon* had sailed from Dunkirk for Ireland. Aboard were 370 French Grenadiers under the command of Napper Tandy, Tone's bitter rival. What it lacked in men the expedition made up for in supplies: guns, cartridges, powder, and a vast armoury of proclamations: 'The soldiers of the GREAT NATION have landed on your coast … JAMES NAPPER TANDY is at their head. He has sworn to lead them on to victory or to die …'.

About a fortnight after Tandy sailed, the French Directory received Humbert's optimistic dispatch. With new respect for their Irish allies, they ordered Hardy not to delay a moment longer.

Tone was at Brest. For once, it seemed, his luck held. This time nothing hindered them, though the expedition that sailed on 16 September was still too small for his liking. Hardy had only succeeded in embarking 2,800 men, distributed in eight frigates, a schooner, and the flagship, the *Hoche*, named for the Frenchman who had led that last armada to Ireland two long years ago.

Humbert had managed, in his masterly way, to throw off his pursuers and keep the initiative. In one march – fifty-eight miles in twenty-four hours – he had reached the outskirts of Sligo. He

won a skirmish at Collooney, an action which earned his opponent, Colonel Vereker, a peerage and the sobriquet 'The Irish Leonidas'. In fact the battle was of little significance, and Humbert pushed on unchecked. But with such a small force as his, he could afford very few Collooneys.

What he needed was allies, but the local people kept their distance. Then, on the evening of 5 September, he heard the long-awaited news: the Midlands had risen. Abandoning his march to Ulster, he set off for Granard, there to link up with the insurgents of Longford and Westmeath. Together, they would march on Dublin. By the evening of the 7th he was only a few miles from County Longford, Cornwallis's cavalry close on his heels. All now depended on whether the rebels could hold out until Humbert reached them.

By 5 September the Westmeath rebels, now about 7,000 strong, had occupied Wilson's Hospital, astride the main road to Longford. The Mullingar garrison left them severely alone, but from Castlepollard, several hours' march to the north, about a hundred yeomanry under Lord Longford set off in pursuit. Reaching the hospital to find the rebels camped all around, they halted and sent urgent word to Cavan for assistance.

Despite the risk of an attack on Cavan, its garrison commander, Major Porter, had set off early that morning with 100 Argyll Fencibles, 250 local yeomanry, and a cannon. In addition to the insurgents at Wilson's Hospital, there were now said to be another 6,000 at Granard, where the rebels made a regular assault. The garrison, re-inforced by Porter's yeomanry, killed 400 rebels – some putting the figure as high as 1,000 – in return for just two of their own men wounded.

At Wilson's Hospital, some of the rebels tried to negotiate a truce. Thousands more deserted. The remainder were trapped between Porter's Highlanders and Longford's yeomanry. About 200 were cut down; others tried to escape across a lake, and many drowned.

Late on the evening of the 7th, all that remained of the United armies of Westmeath and Longford staggered into Humbert's camp at Cloone. No other counties had risen to join them.

The net was now closing around Humbert. Cornwallis had split his army into two; Lake hung on at the enemy's rear; the Viceroy kept his troops between Humbert and the capital. Early next morning all three armies were neck and neck in the race for Dublin, and on that day the race was abruptly ended. Near Ballinamuck Humbert turned and drew up his 850 French troops in line

FAR LEFT: Wolfe Tone in the uniform of a French adjutant-general, as he appeared at his court-martial in Dublin. He had no illusions of what was in store for him.
LEFT: His death mask in his alma mater, Trinity College, Dublin.

of battle. Of the legions of Irish who had joined them, only about a thousand remained. There could be little doubt of the outcome.

Humbert fought for as long as the honour of the Great Nation demanded. Then, as he reported to the Directory with understandable pride: 'After having obtained the greatest successes and made the arms of the French Republic triumph … I have at length been obliged to submit to a superior force of 30,000 men.'

The Irish levies were less fortunate. When Lake's cavalry had finished with them, the bodies of several hundred littered the battlefield and neighbouring bogs.

Cornwallis now arranged the final phase of the campaign. General Trench was to march westward to mop up the remnants of the Franco-Irish army at Castlebar and Killala. Moore was to take station at Moate in Westmeath, ready for any new crisis. The Viceroy had just heard from London that Hardy's expedition had at last sailed.

At Ballinamuck, there were about ninety rebel prisoners, who were soon disposed of, most by hanging. Meanwhile Humbert and his men were being treated with all the courtesy demanded by the conventions of war. Then, fêted by Dublin society, he and his men sailed back to France, released in an exchange of prisoners.

In Killala, however, Dr Stock was still beset by

ABOVE: A rebel ambush in the woods of County Wicklow, from a contemporary print. Led by Michael Dwyer and Joseph Holt, rebels adopted guerrilla war in Wicklow, which took several years to burn itself out.

rebels. Tone and Tandy had not yet tasted the bitterness of their homecoming. The rebellion's last chapter had still to be written.

Mayo, September–October

Nearly a fortnight had passed since news of Ballinamuck had reached Killala. The French officers and Irish loyalists tried to keep the news secret, fearful of its effect upon the insurgents. But soon survivors of the battle made their way back.

Despite the efforts of a young and gallant man, Ferdy O'Donnell, who had replaced the levies' drunken general, the people began to talk of vengeance on the Protestants. The French officers were tireless in their stratagems to prevent trouble. Even so, the loyalists at Killala began increasingly to feel like the loyalists at Wexford. 'We hold our lives by a thread,' the Bishop wrote in his diary.

On 16 September, Napper Tandy sailed into the harbour of Rutland, on the north-western tip of Ireland. His troops disembarked and seized the post office, where peasants assured them that the Mayo rising was in full swing. By chance, however, the postmaster was an old friend of Tandy,

and swiftly told the United man that the rising in Mayo was negligible and that Humbert had surrendered a week before. Tandy maintained a bluff pose, though privately confessing his astonishment at the news of the surrender, and continued to hand out proclamations. He then spent a nostalgic evening with his old friend, after which he was carried insensible to the *Anacréon*. Next morning she sailed, so ending the last landing of a French invasion force on the coasts of the British Isles.

The loyalists at Killala knew nothing of this interlude. They had just learned that Trench had relieved Castlebar – but so had the rebels.

Trench, in fact, knew nothing of the Killala loyalists' predicament. Told by a loyalist envoy, he returned a message that he hoped to be there himself on Sunday with 1,200 men and 5 cannon.

The battle that followed, on 23 September, was the last military action of the rebellion. It was no less tragic than countless others in which half-armed peasants took the field despite hopeless odds. With a force of English and Irish militia and some English dragoons and Scotch Fencibles, Trench pushed on directly towards Killala, while a force of yeomanry and militia moved to take the town from the rear.

For half an hour the rebels made a gallant resistance. Then they broke and fled. Ferdy O'Donnell was killed, but how many others died in the slaughter that followed will never be known. The Bishop estimated it at 400, Trench at 600. As usual, the troops were exasperated, and their officers could not control them. Hunted down like animals, the peasants fled into the wildest parts of Erris, where many died of their wounds or of exposure.

The end of the Mayo rising followed the usual brutal pattern, in spite of the exertions of Trench and his officers, bringing death and destruction to loyalists as well as rebels. Even now the Bishop found no respite. There were courts martial and hangings, and the soldiers lived off the town as if it were enemy country. But at last the troops went, and Mayo was left to itself. As winter approached, famine followed in the wake of revolution.

Dublin and the Three Kingdoms
2 October – 19 November

On 2 October, church bells began to peal victory across the three kingdoms. Nelson had crushed Bonaparte's fleet at the mouth of the Nile without the loss of a single British ship. Hour by hour the news – and wild celebrations – spread across England. By the 5th, that shock wave of rejoicing had reached Ireland. Dublin, the city that felt itself to be most threatened by Bonaparte, was not slow

to celebrate his apparent downfall. In a sense, it was also celebrating the end of the rebellion.

At one stroke, Nelson seemed to have redrawn the map of Europe. The diplomatic possibilities were boundless. The immediate military results, however, were still more dazzling for Britain and Ireland. Bonaparte, so recently the master of Europe, was now marooned in the east. For the time being the Directory must abandon all military ventures against Britain and Ireland.

The Brest fleet still had to be dealt with, however. Then, on 12 October, Rear-Admiral Sir John Warren intercepted Hardy's expedition off the mouth of Lough Swilly, on Ulster's north coast. His victory was, in its way, as complete as Nelson's. Without losing a ship, Warren captured all but two of the French vessels, with 2,500 troops on board – and the gallant Irish commander, adjutant-general Smith, otherwise Wolfe Tone.

It was nearly a month before Tone was brought to Dublin to face a military court. Cornwallis, meanwhile, had lost a battle more decisive than any of the others of that disastrous year.

Despite the Viceroy's ardent protestations, Pitt and the British cabinet, encouraged by the Irish ex-cabinet that Cornwallis had dismissed, agreed to exclude Catholic emancipation from the terms of the Union, for Pitt now believed that, difficult as it would be to steer the Union through on a narrow Protestant basis, it was wholly impractical on broader terms. Besides the almost universal

ABOVE: Joseph Holt, one of the few Protestants who fought with the rebels in Wicklow. He was later transported to Botany Bay. The Irish convicts who survived the voyage soon made up a quarter of Australia's population.

LEFT: Robert Emmet, 24-year-old brother of Thomas Addis Emmet, the United Irish leader. His rising in 1803 brought him to the scaffold.

hostility of the Irish Protestant Parliament, the majority of his own cabinet were opposed to making this concession to the Catholics. By mid-November, Cornwallis had conceded defeat.

The aftermath of the rebellion left Ireland in a state of shock. But, as Cornwallis's new policy of conciliation began to take effect, the cycle of violence slowly worked itself out.

The loyalists, of course, needed no encouragement to condemn this softness, as they saw it, towards the rebels. When Cornwallis publicly rebuked Lord Enniskillen and other members of a court martial for acquitting a yeoman who had deliberately killed a pardoned rebel, the outcry was loud and vicious.

Cornwallis soldiered on. The rebellion, the result of gross misgovernment, had made the Union a matter of strategic necessity for both nations. But whatever payment he would have to make to induce the Irish Parliament to accept it, he was not prepared to pay them in floggings and executions.

Already the loss of life and property had been on a scale unknown in Ireland since the rebellion of 1641. The Castle estimated the total casualties at 20,000, of which some 1,500 were loyalists. Meanwhile, the Autumn Assizes, running in parallel with the courts martial, greatly increased the total sentences of death and transportation. In fact, the death roll was probably much higher. Contemporary evidence suggests 30,000. Men, women and children were murdered, trapped between rival terrors, and on both sides there were numerous deaths from exposure and exhaustion.

The Government received claims totalling £1,023,337 for compensation to the 'suffering loyalists'. Those who were not loyalists, naturally enough, were not compensated. About a dozen towns had been partly or completely destroyed: some by the military, others by the rebels; most by both sides. But as autumn turned to winter the process of reconstruction had already begun, helped by that golden summer, which had produced one of the harvests of the century.

On 8 November, Wolfe Tone was escorted, in irons, into Dublin. He had no illusions as to the fate in store for him.

Early on the 10th crowds began to gather outside the Dublin barracks, anxious for seats at the court martial of the celebrated revolutionary. After a few questions from the President, Tone began to read a statement to the court. He admitted all the charges against him, and asked only one favour – a soldier's death before a firing squad.

LEFT: Thomas Street, Dublin, the scene of Robert Emmet's execution in 1803. Late nineteenth-century engraving.

LEFT:
'The United Irish Patriots of 1798' reincarnated in 1898 for the first centenary of the rebellion. From left to right: S. Neilson, M. Dwyer, J. Sheares, W. Corbet, A. O'Connor (seated), A. H. Rowan, W. Jackson, W. McNevin (seated), M. Teeling, R. Emmet, H. Sheares, T. W. Tone, J. N. Tandy (seated), T. A. Emmet, J. Hope (seated), H J. McCracken (seated), T. Russell, Lord E. Fitzgerald.

Tone spoke from the dock with courage and with dignity. 'What I have done has been clearly from principle and the fullest conviction of its rectitude. I wish not for mercy; I hope I am not an object of pity … The favourite object of my life has been the independence of my country, and to that object I have made every sacrifice.' His sentence – that he should be executed for treason – was inevitable.

His appeal to die by firing squad was rejected. Meanwhile, apparently unknown to him, some friends at the Dublin Bar had devised an ingenious legal scheme for respite. But they were too late. An hour or so before he was due to be executed – and while the feverish attempts to secure the stay were still under way – Wolfe Tone sought a different form of respite. He cut his throat.

Even now his ordeal was not over. The razor had severed his windpipe, instead of his jugular. He died a week later, at the age of thirty-five.

No one knows for certain where he lies buried.

Tone lived long enough to see his dream of a United Ireland dispelled. But if he cannot avoid some of the responsibility for the military catastrophe that his rebellion became, his posthumous achievements have been great and enduring. Not the least of these is that, for later generations of Irishmen, he helped transform what would otherwise have been remembered as a national catastrophe into a heroic struggle of a people against their oppressors, of Irish liberty against English tyranny.

The United Kingdom, France and America, 1 January 1801 and after

The direct result of the rebellion was the Union of Ireland with Britain, officially consummated on 1 January 1801.

The Union controversy split Ireland. In the event, however, the Government's view carried the day, strengthened by unprecedented inducements by way of jobs and peerages, although amongst the mass of the Irish peasantry there was no flicker of interest in the great debates about their nation's future.

Those who had been caught up in the rebellion continued to pay a heavy price. In some districts the violence continued sporadically into 1799. In the country as a whole there was a boom in rents and a slump in employment. The summer was wet and in many areas the harvest failed. Famine threatened.

The result was a wave of emigration to England and Scotland, rising soon to an average of 50,000 a year. But like all poor emigrants, the Irish had to take the worst jobs and live in the worst ghettos. Their offspring went out to work as child labourers.

RIGHT: Miles Byrne, apparently the only United Irish leader to survive into the age of photography. He died in 1860, after a distinguished career in the French army.

The political prisoners sent abroad generally suffered even worse. Those pressed into the services – including the Prussian army – fared worse still.

Other political prisoners were transported to the penal colony at Botany Bay; indeed, by 1802 Irishmen made up a quarter of its population. In due course some of them were released and found their way back to Ireland. Today there is a war memorial in Sydney to the men of '98.

In January 1799, the third group of political prisoners – the seventy-eight United Irish leaders who had signed the 'Treaty of Newgate' with the Government – were still in custody. At the Peace of Amiens in 1802 they were allowed to banish themselves to France.

Next year renewed hostilities regenerated hopes that the French would help liberate Ireland. The leader of this second revolutionary movement was Thomas Addis Emmet's 24-year-old brother, Robert, who had escaped to France shortly before the rebellion. The older United Irish leaders were unenthusiastic; so were the ordinary Irish people. The rising ended in a scuffle in the Dublin streets; Robert Emmet's life, on the scaffold.

By 1805 Britain's naval supremacy, which was finally confirmed at Trafalgar, had put an end to all hopes of French assistance. The survivors of the United Irish Executive now separated. Thomas Addis Emmet, Neilson and McNevin, among others, went to America to find positions which were more congenial to their talents. And most succeeded triumphantly.

Fortune also smiled on the United Irish who stayed in France. Lewins, Lawless and others all prospered, many as soldiers fighting against their own compatriots in the British armies. But the United Irishman who achieved the highest honours in the French army never saw a shot fired. Arthur O'Connor retired contentedly to a château with the rank and pay of a general-of-division, dying tranquilly in 1852 at the dawn of the Second Empire.

It soon emerged that the Union was not what its champions had hoped, or its opponents had feared. Cornwallis was right: it was merely a union with the Protestant party in Ireland.

Perversely, this party had put up the most vigorous fight against it. But, finding they were not after all to be stripped of their power, they soon returned to the fold.

The other main group of anti-Unionists – the liberal opposition – were also swiftly reconciled with the Government. Even the great Henry

LEFT: 'Hunted Down' (1885). By the time of the first '98 centenary the rebellion was remembered not as a horrific civil war but as a simple story of a people's struggle against their oppressors.

Grattan took his seat in London with the British Whigs and declared the Union to be irreversible.

By contrast, the main sponsors of the Union found their hopes blighted. Pitt had planned to end the Catholic question once and for all by giving Catholics complete political equality with Protestants. As soon as the Union was passed, he had begun preparations. But the Irish Protestants saw Catholic emancipation as political suicide, and, encouraged by the King, formed an alliance with their British counterparts in the United Parliament to block it. Pitt was forced to resign – the first, but by no means the last British Prime Minister to be broken by the Irish Question. His partners in Ireland – Cornwallis, Castlereagh and Cooke – resigned in sympathy.

The Union failed for many reasons, including the way it was imposed and the tenacity of Irish nationalism. If it had been followed by the Catholic concessions which Pitt had planned, it might have had a chance. Instead, the Protestant Irish retained their political monopoly, and the British Government their inertia. The Union did, however, endure in the one part of Ireland where Protestants had a majority – the six (originally nine) counties of Ulster.

And in Ulster today, the ghosts of '98 have still not been laid to rest.

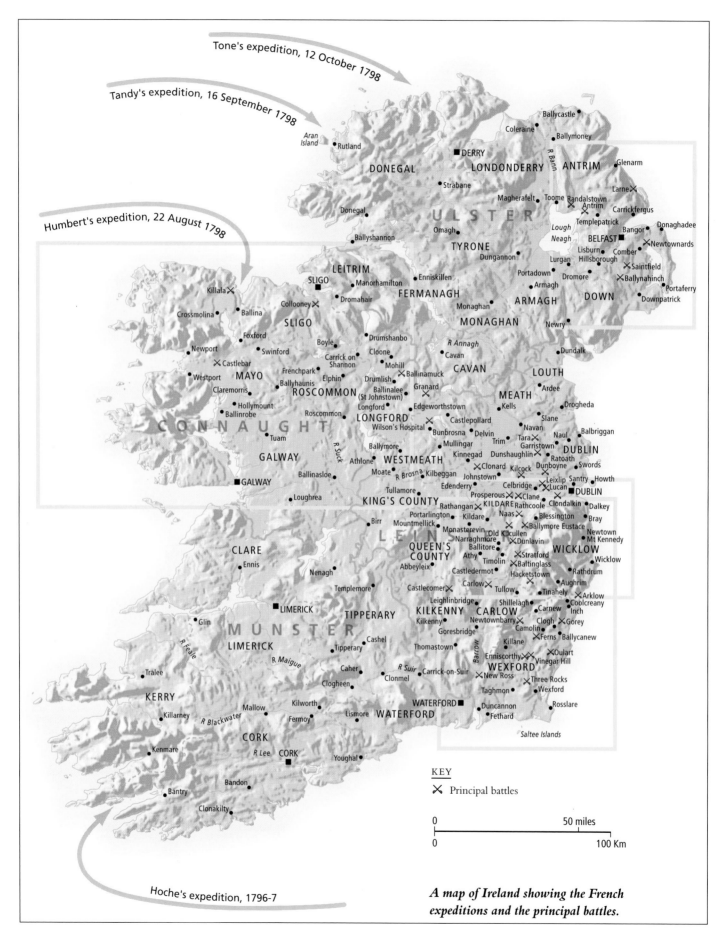

Tone's expedition, 12 October 1798

Tandy's expedition, 16 September 1798

Humbert's expedition, 22 August 1798

Hoche's expedition, 1796-7

Aran Island
Rutland

DONEGAL
■ DERRY
LONDONDERRY
R Bann
ANTRIM
Glenarm
Ballycastle
Coleraine
Ballymoney
Strabane
Magherafelt
Toome
Randalstown
Antrim
Larne ✕
Carrickfergus
U L S T E R
Templepatrick
Bangor
Donaghadee
Donegal
Omagh
Lough Neagh
BELFAST ■
Newtownards
Ballyshannon
TYRONE
Dungannon
Lurgan
Lisburn
Hillsborough
Comber
LEITRIM
Manorhamilton
Enniskillen
Portadown
Dromore
Saintfield ✕
SLIGO ■
Dromahair
FERMANAGH
Armagh
Ballynahinch ✕
Killala ✕
Colaoney ✕
Monaghan
ARMAGH
DOWN
Portaferry
Crossmolina
Ballina
Foxford
Drumshanbo
R Annagh
MONAGHAN
Newry
Downpatrick
Newport
Swinford
Boyle
Cloone
Cavan
CAVAN
LOUTH
Dundalk
Castlebar ✕
Frenchpark
Carrick on Shannon
Mohill
Ballinamuck ✕
Ardee
Westport
MAYO
Ballyhaunis
Elphin
Drumlish
Granard ✕
MEATH
Kells
Drogheda
Claremorris
ROSCOMMON
Ballinalee (St Johnstown) ✕
Edgeworthstown
Slane
Hollymount
Longford
Castlepollard
Navan
Balbriggan
Ballinrobe
Roscommon
LONGFORD
Wilson's Hospital ✕
Bunbrosna
Delvin
Tara ✕
Naul
Tuam
C O N N A U G H T
R Suck
Ballymore
Mullingar
Trim
Garristown
DUBLIN
Ratoath
Athlone
WESTMEATH
Kinnegad
Dunshaughlin
Dunboyne ✕
Swords
Santry
Howth
GALWAY
Moate
R Brosna
Kilbeggan
Johnstown
Clonard ✕
Kilcock ✕
Leixlip ✕
Lucan
DUBLIN ✕
Ballinasloe
Tullamore
Edenderry
Celbridge
Clane ✕
GALWAY ■
KING'S COUNTY
Prosperous
Rathangan ✕
KILDARE ✕
Clane ✕
Rathcoole
Clondalkin
Dalkey
Loughrea
Birr
Rathangan ✕
Kildare
Naas ✕
Blessington
Bray
Portarlington
Mountmellick
Monasterevin
Old Kilcullen
Ballymore Eustace
Newtown Mt Kennedy
CLARE
Narraghmore
Kilcullen ✕
Dunlavin
WICKLOW
Ennis
L E I N S T E R
QUEEN'S COUNTY
Ballitore
Stratford
Wicklow
Nenagh
Athy
Timolin
Baltinglass ✕
Rathdrum
Abbeyleix
Castledermot
Hacketstown ✕
Aughrim
Templemore
Carlow ✕
Tullow
Tinahely
Arklow ✕
LIMERICK ■
Castlecomer ✕
Coolcreany
Leighlinbridge
Shillelagh
Carnew
Inch
TIPPERARY
KILKENNY
CARLOW
Clogh ✕ Gorey
Glin
Kilkenny
Newtownbarry ✕
Camolin
Ballycanew
M U N S T E R
Goresbridge
Ferns ✕
Cashel
Thomastown
Killane
Oulart ✕
LIMERICK
R Maigue
Tipperary
R Barrow
Enniscorthy ✕
Vinegar Hill ✕
Caher
R Suir
Carrick-on-Suir
WEXFORD
Clogheen
Clonmel
New Ross ✕
Three Rocks ✕
Tralee
R Feale
Kilworth
Lismore
WATERFORD ■
Taghmon
Wexford
KERRY
Mallow
Fermoy
WATERFORD
Duncannon
Rosslare
Killarney
R Blackwater
Fethard
Kenmare
CORK
Youghal
Saltee Islands
R Lee
CORK ■
Bantry
Bandon
Clonakilty

KEY

✕ Principal battles

0   50 miles
0   100 Km

A map of Ireland showing the French
expeditions and the principal battles.

A Chronology of the Significant Events of the Year 1798

January 22 Proclaiming of Queen's County to be in a state of insurrection.

February 26 General Abercromby's order denouncing the Irish army as 'formidable to everyone but the enemy'.

February 28 Arrest of United Irish leaders Arthur O'Connor and Fr. Quigley at Margate, Kent.

March 12 Arrest of 16 United Irish leaders, including the Leinster Executive at Oliver Bond's, cripples the movement.

March 26 Abercromby forced to resign, with effect from mid-April.

March 30 Proclamation of martial law, to be followed by free quarters in disturbed districts.

March–April Lent assizes: about 100 convictions in Midlands and the South.

Mid-April Abercromby supervises free quarters in Tipperary, Kildare.more violent measures to detect and disarm the conspiracy.

Early May New United Irish Executive led by John Sheares and John Lawless with Neilson and Lord Edward Fitzgerald in the background. Plan for coup without waiting for French assistance.

May 1 Violent measures to disarm Kildare. United men begin in Athy.

May 12 Proclamation of £1000 reward for arrest of Lord Edward Fitzgerald.

May 13 Ultimatum for surrender of arms in Wicklow.

May 18 Trial of Earl of Kingston in Dublin. Split in United Execu-tive: Sheares brothers resign, Lawless flees.

May 19 Arrest of Lord Edward Fitzgerald, after struggle in which he kills Ryan and is himself fatally wounded.

May 20 Climax of disarming in N. Kildare and N. Wicklow. Magan's report of impending insurrection.

May 20 Flogging of suspects at Tinahely (Wicklow) begins.

May 21 Arrest of Sheares brothers with incriminating papers.

May 21–22 (Maidstone) Trial of Arthur O'Connor, etc. Fr. Quigley condemned to be hanged.

May 22 Start of disarming of suspects in Dublin by yeomanry.

May 23 Sproule's report: 'they will rise tonight'. Arrest of Neilson.

May 23 Pitch-capping of Anthony Perry and other violent measures in Wexford. Flogging at Carnew, Gorey, Camolin and Ballycanew.

May 23/24 Rising begins with

co-ordinated attacks on Dunshaughlin and Dunboyne (Meath), Clondalkin (Co. Dublin), Clane, Prosperous and Naas (Kildare). Attacks repulsed. Crown forces lose 50 men at Prosperous, 22 at Naas, otherwise suffer few casualties. United forces lose over 200. But burning of Mail coaches at Santry (Dublin) and outside Naas (Kildare) sends signal of insurrection.

May 24 Attack on Old Kilcullen kills 30 soldiers, at a cost of 150 United men. General Dundas retires, leaving much of Kildare to be occupied by United army.

May 24 Camden's SOS to London for British reinforcements. Proclamation and order to surrender arms, followed by solemn declaration of loyalty by leading Catholics (late May).

May 24/25 Attacks on Carlow, Hacketstown and the Wicklow garrisons at Ballymore, Dunlavin, Stratford and Baltinglass. Attacks beaten off, streets choked with United dead.

May 25 Abortive attacks on Lucan (Co. Dublin), Kilcock (Meath) and Leixlip (Kildare). United forces regroup at Dunboyne camp.

May 25/26 Brutal execution by Crown forces of 28 prisoners at Dunlavin (Wicklow) and 28 more at Carnew (Wexford) spreads terror southwards.

May 26 Rathangan overrun by 'Defenders' killing garrison.

WEXFORD

May 26 Rumours of United victories in Kildare reach Wexford. Rising in Wexford begins, led by Fr. John Murphy of Boulavogue and Fr. Michael Murphy of Ballycanew. Killing of Lieutenant Bookey and Camolin yeomanry, Revd Burrowes and others.

May 26/27 In reprisal, yeomanry burn Fr. John Murphy's house and chapel at Oulart.

May 27 Annihilation of Colonel Foote and 100 men of N. Cork militia at Oulart. Loyalists retreat from Gorey to Arklow.

May 28 Rebels capture Ferns and burn town.

MEATH

May 27 Battle of Tara. Crown forces destroy United army, killing about 350 insurgents for the loss of about 13 killed and 28 wounded on their own side. Road to the North reopened.

KILDARE

May 28 General Dundas personally accepts surrender of 3,000 rebels at Knockallen Hill. General Duff relieves Kildare town.

May 28 Recapture of Rathangan by Crown forces.

May 31 Massacre of 350 rebels, when coming in to surrender, at Gibbet Rath.

WEXFORD

May 28 Led by Fr. John Murphy, United army captures Enniscorthy, killing over 100 men of the garrison. Survivors flee to Wexford.

May 30 United army's victories at the Three Rocks. Wexford garrison abandons Wexford to rebels.

June 1 Crown forces repulse United army's attack on Newtownbarry (Bunclody) and thus prevent them advancing into Carlow.

June 4 United army captures Gorey.

June 5 Battle of New Ross. United army, led by Bagenal Harvey, loses over 2,000 men and fails to break out into Kilkenny and Waterford. Massacre of 200 loyalist prisoners at Scullabogue and later at Vinegar Hill camp.

ANTRIM

June 7 Battle of Antrim. United army led by Henry Joy McCracken. But attacks on Antrim and Larne repulsed, and 300 United men killed. Randalstown and Ballymena briefly occupied by rebels, then recaptured.

June 11 United camp at Donegore Hill abandoned. Henry Joy McCracken escapes but is later caught and hanged.

DOWN

June 9 United army surprise Crown forces, then capture Saintfield and Newtownards. Camp formed at Ballynahinch under leadership of Monro.

June 13 Battle of Ballynahinch. General Nugent crushes United army, killing over 300 men. Monro captured and later hanged.

WEXFORD

June 9 Battle of Arklow. United army, led by Fr. John Murphy, loses 300–400 men and fails to break out into Wicklow and head for Dublin.

June 20 Massacre of about 90 loyalist prisoners at Wexford bridge.

June 21 General Lake's combined forces storm Vinegar Hill and crush 20,000-strong United army under Fr. Philip Roche. Government atrocities including burning of rebel hospital at Enniscorthy. Wexford recaptured. But several thousand United men escape.

June 21 and after. Execution of United leaders, including Fr.

Roche, Mathew Keogh and B. B. Harvey. Widespread atrocities by Crown forces.

THE MIDLANDS AND SOUTH

June 22 Lord Cornwallis replaces Lord Camden as Lord Lieutenant.

June 21–27 Abortive attempts by surviving Wexford United men, led by Fr. John Murphy, Perry and Fitzgerald, to link up with Kildare United remnants.

June 23 Battle of Castlecomer.

June 25 Battle of Hacketstown.

July 10 Perry's force finally reaches Kildare but fails to reignite rebellion.

July 11 Attack on Clonard repulsed.

July 20 Surrender of Aylmer and Kildare rebels at Timahoe under conditional amnesty for leaders.

July 20 Execution of Perry and Fr. Kearns at Edenderry.

DUBLIN

July 12–25 Four United leaders – Henry and John Sheares, McCann and Byrne – tried, and executed at Newgate.

July 26 Remaining United leaders under arrest agree 'treaty' with Government, admitting their part in the plan for revolution.

OUTSIDE DUBLIN

August 22 General Humbert lands with French invasion force of 1,099 men at Killala, precipitating Mayo rising.

August 27 Humbert defeats Lake's 1,700 men at the Races of Castlebar. Hundreds of militia desert.

September 4–6 Longford and Westmeath risings in hopes of linking with French, but crushed at Granard and Wilson's Hospital, with at least 600 men killed.

September 5 Humbert makes for Dublin after minor victory at Colooney.

September 8 Battle of Ballinamuck. Hundreds of United men killed, 90 taken prisoner. Humbert surrenders to Cornwallis. Execution of many Irish taken prisoner.

September 16 Napper Tandy lands at Rutland, Donegal, from French frigate *Anacréon*, but re-embarks (drunk) after a few hours.

September 23 Recapture of Killala and collapse of Mayo rising. Atrocities by Crown forces.

October 16 British squadron under Admiral Warren defeats Bompard's expedition, with Wolfe Tone on board the *Hoche*.

DUBLIN

November 10 Wolfe Tone condemned by court martial but cuts his throat to avoid execution.

1.

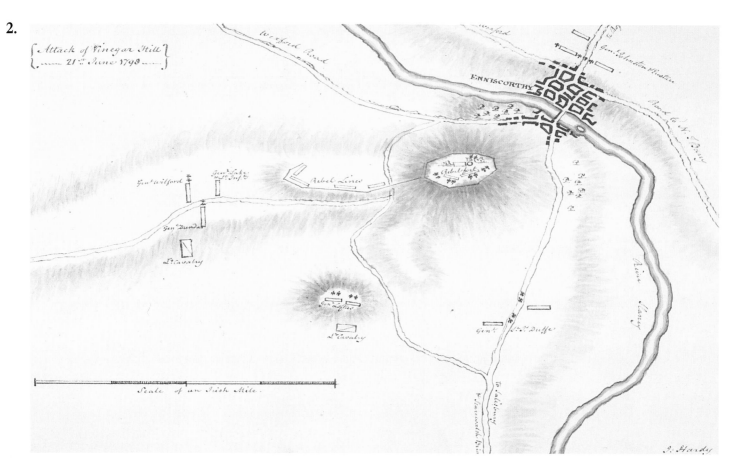

KEY

○ United forces

△ Government forces

↗ United forces direction of attack

▢ Occupied area

DUBLIN

■ DUBLIN

Tara ↑

Kilcock

Maynooth

Leixlip

Edenderry

Timahoe

Celbridge

R Liffey

KING'S COUNTY (OFFALY)

Prosperous

Clane

Rathangan

KILDARE

Curragh

Naas

Kildare

Kilcullen Bridge

Gibbet Rath

Blackmore

Monasterevin

Old Kilcullen

Ballymore Eustace

WICKLOW

R Barrow

Narraghmore

Athy

Ballitore

QUEEN'S COUNTY (LAOIS)

Mail coach road to Cork ↓

CARLOW

Carlow

0 ────── 10 miles
0 ────── 20 Km

2.

{Attack of Vinegar Hill
21st June 1798}

Wexford Road

ENNISCORTHY

Rebel Line

Scale of an Irish Mile.

J. Hardy

1. May 26
*Midlands front
showing the
approximate areas
occupied by the
United Armies of
Kildare, Wicklow
and Meath.*

3.

2. June 21
*A contemporary
plan of the battle
of Vinegar Hill,
outside
Enniscorthy.*

3. June 4
*Wexford and
South East
Leinster showing
the approximate
area occupied by
United forces.*

Naas

Bray

Kildare

Kilcullen

Blessington

Monasterevin

Ballymore Eustace

KILDARE

WICKLOW

QUEEN'S
COUNTY
(LAOIS)

Dunlavin
May 25

Ballitore

Stratford
on Slaney

Athy

Wicklow

Baltinglass

Rathdrum

Rathvilly

Hacketstown

Aughrim

Carlow

Tinahely
May 20

Tullow

Arklow
May 21

CARLOW

Shillelagh

Inch
May 23

Oldleighlin

Leighlinbridge

Clonegall

Carnew
May 26

Kilkenny

Gorey
May 23

Newtown
Barry
(Bunclody)

Camolin
May 25

← Mail coach
road to Cork

Goresbridge

Ballycanew
May 25

Borris

Ferns

The Harrow
Boolavogue

KILKENNY

Enniscorthy
May 25

Oulart

WEXFORD

New Ross

Old Ross

Mid May

Taghmon

Foulksmill

Wexford

WATERFORD

Duncannon

Saltee Islands

KEY

⊗ Towns where Govt
atrocities reported

County boundary

☐ Occupied area

Strategic roads

△ Government
garrisons

⬡ Strategic hill-top
camps.

| 0 | | 10 miles |
| 0 | | 20 Km |

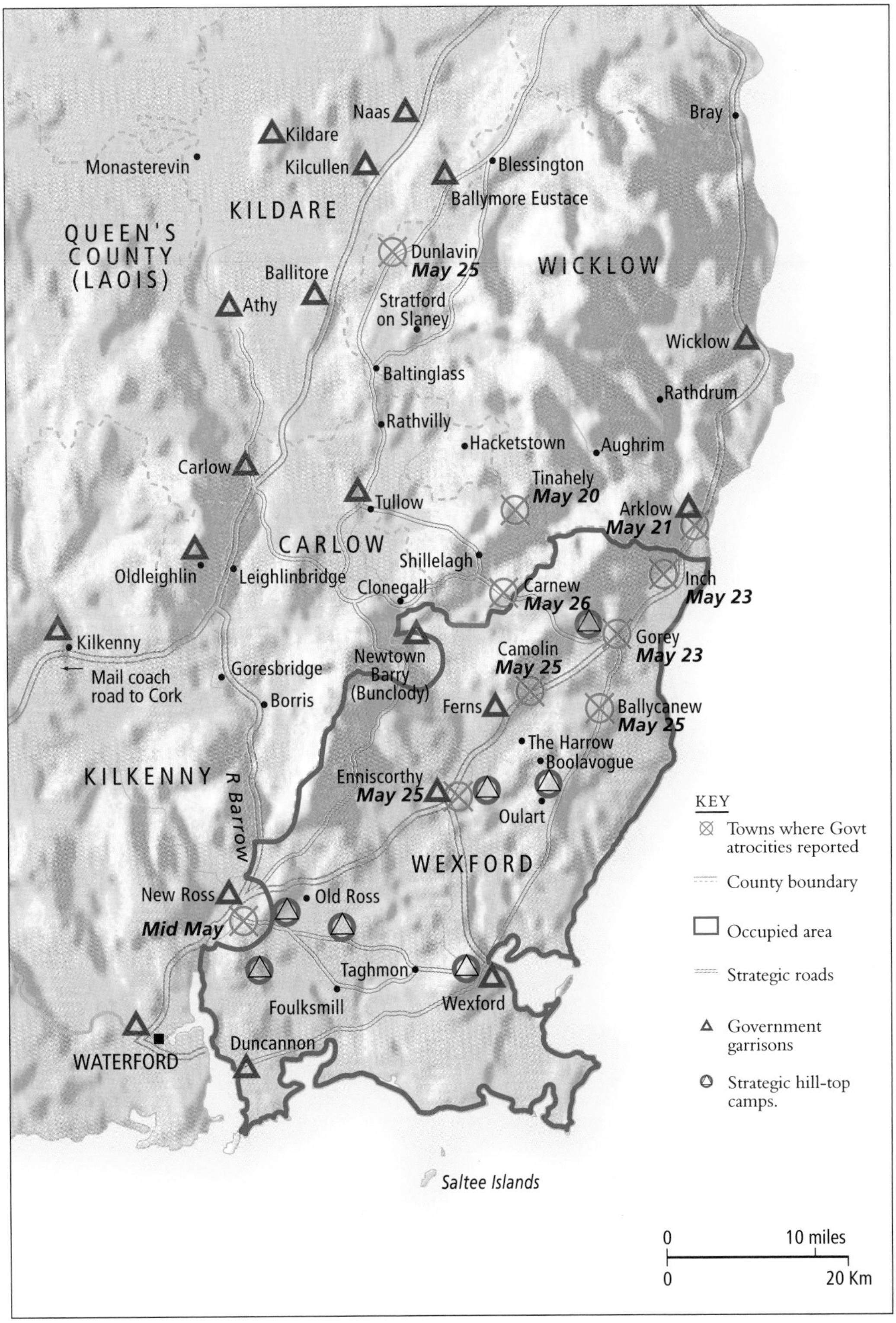

4.

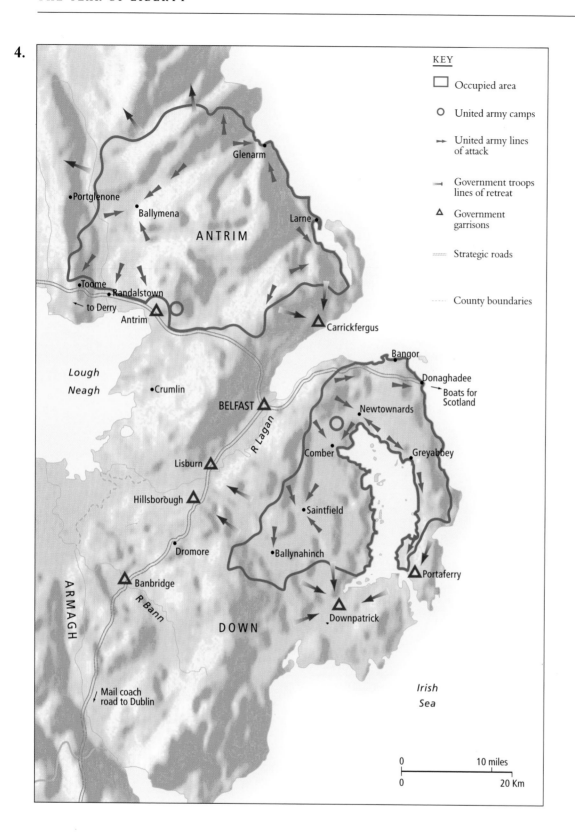

KEY

☐ Occupied area

○ United army camps

⊶ United army lines of attack

⊢ Government troops lines of retreat

△ Government garrisons

═══ Strategic roads

───── County boundaries

4. June 8/9
North-east Ulster,
showing the
approximate area
occupied by the
United armies of
Down and Antrim.

5. September 4
The western front
at dawn, showing
the approximate
area of Mayo
occupied by the
French.

6. September 8
A contemporary
plan showing the
positions of the
English and
French armies at
Ballinamuck at
the time of the
French surrender.

5.

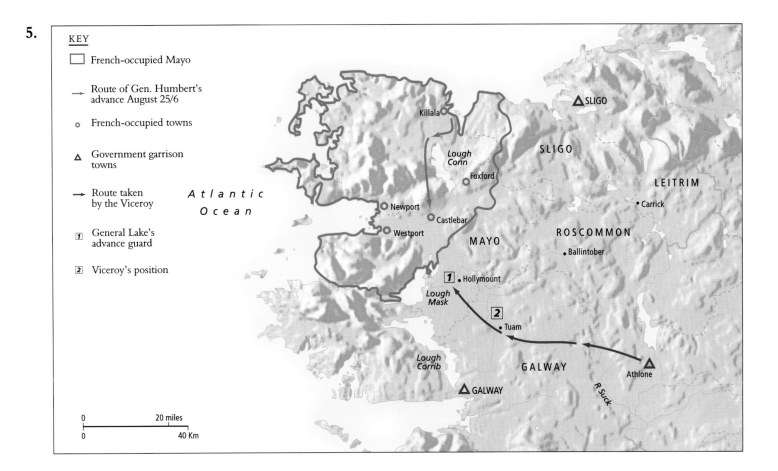

KEY

▭ French-occupied Mayo

→ Route of Gen. Humbert's advance August 25/6

○ French-occupied towns

△ Government garrison towns

→ Route taken by the Viceroy

☐1 General Lake's advance guard

☐2 Viceroy's position

6.

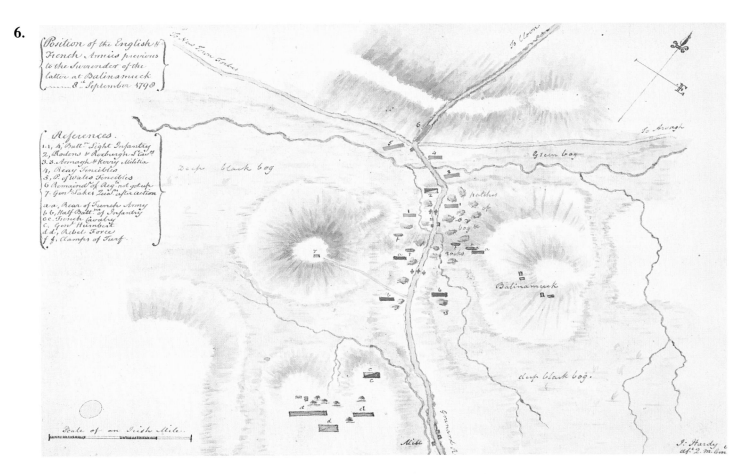

THE BATTLE AT WEXFORD

Between his Majesty's Forces and the Rebel Army when the Rebels were defeated with great slaughter and most

Published July 17. 1798 by I. Marshall No 7.